A SAILOR'S WAR

W. G. Mattin

GW00545882

ARTHUR H. STOCKWELL LTD
Torrs Park, Ilfracombe, Devon, EX34 8BA
Established 1898
www.ahstockwell.co.uk

British Library Cataloguing-in-Publication Data.
A catalogue record for this book is available
from the British Library.

Arthur H. Stockwell Ltd bears no responsibility
for the accuracy of information recorded in this book.

ISBN 978-0-7223-4201-5
Printed in Great Britain by
Arthur H. Stockwell Ltd
Torrs Park   Ilfracombe
Devon   EX34 8BA

CONTENTS

FOREWORD

It was a remarkable coincidence. I had been at the spot five years previously – it could have been almost to the very day. It was a double coincidence really, because this ship, the first warship I had ever set foot on (as a member of a working party from the nearby barracks), was also going to be the last one I stepped off.

It was January 1946, and HMS *London* was tied up alongside in Chatham Dockyard. This ship had brought us on the last stage of our journey home from the Far East to our port division, HMS *Pembroke*, for demobilisation.

The bosun's pipe had just shrilled out over the Tannoy, followed by the order "All ratings on draft to the barracks, fall in on the port side."

As we stood with our kitbags and hammocks, waiting for the order to disembark, my mind went back over that five years. Much had happened during that time. I had travelled many thousands of miles and witnessed many incidents – some quite amusing, others tragic and very frightening.

The 'action' had begun for me somewhere between Alexandria and Malta, with 15th Cruiser Squadron, 'The Fighting 15th'.

CHAPTER 1

"MALTA CONVOY, STAND TO!"

The order, passed down by phone from the turret and repeated by Petty Officer Wilson, captain of the magazine, had an ominous ring about it. It meant that action was imminent.

The talking ceased abruptly as we grabbed shells and charges and took up our positions at the hoists. We had heard the pump start up above us, and the turret and its trunk began to train round. Any second now, the hoists would start their infernal clattering as the turret opened fire.

The ship trembled slightly as the engine revolutions were increased. We could only guess what was happening up top – probably an aircraft had come in sight.

It was a twin 5.25-inch turret, and the ship had five of these. Shells and charges were separate – the former weighing eighty pounds, and the latter twenty. The guns had a very high elevation and could put a shell up to about 50,000 feet. Rate of fire was approximately twelve to fifteen rounds per minute.

Petty Officer Wilson stood with the handset close to his ear. All eyes were upon him – every man tense and waiting.

"On your toes, lads!"

An instant later, the hoists clattered into life. All was action now – the waiting and wondering was over. Only one thing mattered now: to get shells and charges into the hoists as quickly as possible.

"Keep those projees [projectiles] and charges coming!" Petty Officer Wilson bellowed at us over the racket of the hoists.

He needn't have worried – we were a well-tried team by now. There was no confusion. We just needed to watch we didn't get in one another's way as the turret revolved.

Suddenly, the ship began to keel over – quite alarmingly, it seemed. Some shells and charges clattered to the deck.

'We are turning under full rudder,' I thought.

Then came a series of crashing explosions – like someone hitting the hull with a great sledgehammer. I could hear the shells 'dancing' in their racks.

The ship lurched to one side, and I almost lost my balance. It took two attempts to get the charge I was holding into the hoist.

"Come on – come on!" Petty Officer Wilson was screaming in my ear. "If that chief gunner's mate up top finds a bubble in the hoists [a shell with no charge] he'll be down here and crucify you!"

More explosions followed, not so loud this time. I briefly caught Stripey's eye.

"Miles away!" he shouted. "Bloody miles away!"

'Some poor devils are copping it,' I thought. 'I wonder what is happening out there.'

Almost immediately came some massive hammer blows on the hull. The ship lurched and shuddered, and I would swear to this day that the cordite racks opposite me bulged in and out again.

Anxious eyes met across the magazine – chalk-white faces, all of them with tightly clenched lips.

Stripey was roaring like a bull. He glanced upwards and shouted, "You Nazi bastard! I hope this shell blows your bloody arse off!"

He literally threw it into the hoist.

"Get in there, projee, and up to that turret in double-quick time!"

"Go easy with those projees, Stripey," Petty Officer Wilson bawled at him. "We don't want them going off down here!"

I thought the remark quite amusing, in an odd kind of way. We wouldn't have known anything about it, would we? There was no danger of that happening really. Although the AA shells we were loading had their fuses fitted, they were not 'set' until the shell reached the turret, and were only then activated when the shell left the gun.

These mechanical fuses had a sliding ring, which was turned to the setting chosen by one of the turret crew. Later on, proximity fuses came along. They incorporated a minute radar, which activated the fuse when the shell reached close proximity to an aircraft.

Magazine crews were drawn from miscellaneous branches. There were usually some seamen among them. Others might be Supply Branch ratings, writers and stewards, etc. It was cold and dark down there – a miserable place to be.

Stripey Mansfield and Alby Clarke were our shell loaders. Another lad and I loaded the charges, and the remainder of the crew kept us supplied.

Stripey, a two-badge AB, was a tough, happy-go-lucky type. Nothing seemed to worry him too much, and he was a tower of strength to us younger lads.

Alby Clarke was sullen, foul-mouthed and argumentative. None of us liked him. The lad who passed the shells to him was frequently subjected to a stream of abuse.

The Petty Officer would interfere sometimes: "Leave the kid alone, and attend to your job."

"I'll sort Alby out, one of these times," Stripey said to me. "I'll fill his bloody face in," he added.

"I will look forward to that," I replied.

Shells were stored in the centre of the magazine, standing upright in three racks, one above the other. The charges in their brass cylinders were stored horizontally, in racks on each side of the magazine. A spring clip held them in place, and a special tool was used to unclip them and draw them out.

On several occasions, when there was a bit of a lull during long periods of action, we unclipped several charges in one row, drew them half out and had a lie-down. An extra bit of luxury was to draw one out in the next row for a pillow! It was not very comfortable really when we were feeling absolutely exhausted, but it was better than standing, or squatting in a corner. Petty

Officer Wilson would give us a 'rocket' sometimes.

"Not too many of those charges out now!"

Entrance to the magazine was by way of a vertical ladder in one corner, leading to a square hatch which was always kept tightly closed. There were iron gratings on the deck, and toilet arrangements were by courtesy of a bucket, secured in one corner. It would have been difficult to find a more cheerless or depressing place.

During temporary lulls in long periods of action, the clips on the hatch would be knocked off, and large containers of soup or cocoa would be passed down to us, together with cheese, ham or corned-beef rolls. These were occasions for rejoicing!

"Nice to know some blighter remembered we are still down here," Stripey would say with a grin.

Shells were loaded into the hoists horizontally, and the charges vertically. The cordite hoists were fitted with a tall, narrow door, which was slammed shut after each charge was pushed in. The 5.25-inch had a high rate of fire, and by the time I had grabbed another charge from Gordon, my supplier, the door had sprung open again.

In charge, slam the door, then reset – and so it went on. Up in the turret – several decks above us, at the other end of the hoists – four other lads of the turrets' crews would be grabbing the shells and charges and placing them in the loading trays. The tray would go over and the ram would come up; the breech closed and the gun fired.

'A bit cramped up there,' I thought.

The 5.25-inch turret was not all that big, and there were a dozen or so blokes in the crew. At least their floor revolved with them – they didn't have to keep moving round like we did.

The turret and trunk containing the hoists was one unit – as the turret trained round, so did the trunk. When the guns were tracking a fast-moving aircraft, there would be a considerable and rapid change of bearing. We in the magazine might find ourselves loading the ammunition on one side of the ship one minute and on the opposite side the next. It could be quite a tiring job.

"It would be a lot easier", I joked to the magazine captain one day, "if the turret kept on a steady bearing."

"Quite right, lad," he replied; "and if those Jerries up top kept in one place, it would be easier to shoot the bastards down!"

We had arrived at Alexandria at a very critical and worrying time. The situation in the Eastern Mediterranean, and with the desert army, was becoming desperate. Since the Germans had arrived on the scene, things had gone from bad to worse, for us. Most of the coastline on both sides of the Med had been in enemy hands since the evacuation of our troops from Greece and the island of Crete. Malta was under siege, and could only be kept supplied at a high cost in men and ships.

It was a convoy operation we were engaged upon now. We had to pass through 'Bomb Alley', as we called it, often under fierce and sustained air attacks by high-level, torpedo and dive bombers, with little or no air cover of our own.

There was also the constant threat of attack by the Italian Fleet. Italy had quite a powerful navy, but never at any time showed much willingness to engage our forces.

A small force of destroyers was based at Malta, and we would meet up with these, fifty miles or so to the east of the island, hand over the supply ships to them, and take empty ones back to Alexandria. Often the changeover would take place under a fierce air attack.

Those few fast supply ships and their crews did a wonderful job, but we were to lose them one by one. One in particular we escorted several times, but sadly she was also lost in the end. I remember seeing her emerge from a forest of bomb splashes apparently unscathed on several occasions when my action station was on pom-poms.

The expenditure of ammunition on these operations was colossal, and sometimes our ships' magazines would get dangerously low.

It was vital that Malta should survive, especially as a base from which our own forces could attack supply convoys supporting Rommel's army. Severe losses were inflicted upon these convoys at times, and this of course helped to relieve the pressure on our desert army. If Malta had fallen, it was a certainty that the whole of the Middle East would have been lost. The whole course of the war would have been changed.

'What must it be like in that turret up there?' I wondered. 'They must feel it much more than we do when the ship keels over like this. It must be murder loading the guns. They are shut up in a steel box also, and cannot see anything, or know what is happening, but at least they have some chance of getting out if the ship is badly hit and begins to sink. Maybe they wouldn't, though, on second thoughts. A bomb could fall directly on to the turret.'

That had happened to the cruiser *Orion* during the evacuation of Crete. There was a direct hit on 'A' turret, which was blown over the side. The blast also killed all the crew of 'B' turret, and actually bent the barrels of the six-inch guns.

HMS *Orion* was packed with troops – over 1,000, I believe. She was repeatedly attacked by both high-level and dive bombers, and was hit four times. One of the 1,000-pound bombs went down through the bridge and exploded on the stokers' mess deck. The result was indescribably terrible.

She limped back to Alexandria with only one screw turning and with a heavy list. Several fires were burning, and she was being steered by her after steering wheel – orders being passed from the bridge by a chain of men.

For several days after her arrival at Alexandria, parties of men from other ships went aboard to clean up. It was a terrible experience – more than 600 men had been killed or injured.

She was patched up, then left the station for permanent repair. It was said that some more human remains were found while this work was in progress.

I wrenched my mind away from these morbid thoughts. 'Concentrate on that little door,' I thought. 'That is the only thing that matters in the world at this moment.'

In charge, slam the door shut, next charge, and the next . . .

My arms were beginning to ache, and each charge was now

a major effort. They only weighed twenty pounds, but had to be lifted to about head height.

'We must have fired a lot of rounds by now,' I thought, and a quick glance at the cordite racks opposite me confirmed this. 'Those enormous explosions I just heard: maybe the ship has been hit?' Our turret was still firing, but that did not tell us anything really. 'If the turret is hit, will we get a flash down here?' I wondered.

The *Orion*'s 'A' turret had been blown off – I wondered what had happened to the magazine crew. It is difficult to say where the safest place might have been. If your action station was above deck, you would have some chance of getting off if the ship was hit and rolled over. If that were to happen, we would have no chance down where we were.

What was it the *Damage Control Handbook* said? *In the event of the ship being torpedoed, you will hear (1) the explosion. What to do: stay where you are, and listen.*

'That's a laugh,' I thought. 'We might be already dead – we certainly would be if the magazine went up.'

You will hear (2) the 'still' on the bugle, or bosun's pipe. What to do: stay put.

You will hear (3) 'damage-control parties close up! Close all red and blue openings!' What to do: if not damage control, stay put.

You will hear (4) the 'carry on', followed by divisions, repel aircraft, or action stations. What to do: if not closed up, walk to the upper deck.

'Bloody hilarious that one,' I thought. 'That one little hatch above could be buckled and impossible to open. Anyway, we might not still be here – we might have been washed out of the ship's side by then!'

More cheerful information followed, I recalled: *The lights may go out, and the ship may list badly. There will be shouting and confusion, unless you keep your head and stop and think. Above all, do not panic.*

'Panic? What's the point of panicking down in this dungeon? There's no bloody place to run to. At least we are safe from near misses down here. Take the pom-pom crews up on the boom deck, for instance. There would be a hail of splinters from a near miss, and they have no protection whatsoever around their mountings.'

I was going to be in a position to experience this a few weeks later, as it turned out.

It seemed to be the practice to move the newer lads round a bit – to give them experience of different jobs, I expect, and also to see what they were most suited to.

"Check! Check! Check!" Petty Officer Wilson had been talking to the turret. "Stand down, lads," he said quietly, "but don't doze off."

The hoists had stopped, and it suddenly became quite peaceful.

"Thank the Lord for that," said Stripey. "I'm bloody knackered," he added.

Sounds of movement came from above – the clips were being knocked off the hatch. The cover was thrown back, and a grinning face peered down at us.

"Are you rats all right down there?" the owner called. "We have brought you some char and rolls."

He was from the damage-control team whose station was just above us. Several of these teams were stationed around the ship at various points.

The damage-control teams were parties of specially trained men, drawn from various branches. Their purpose was, according to the *Damage Control Handbook*, to enable the ship to float – to steam and to fight, in spite of damage. It was their job to give the initial 'first aid', but of course it was also the responsibility of everyone to know something about damage control. For that reason it was stressed very strongly that we should know our part of the ship thoroughly – such things as knowing what every pipe passing through a compartment was carrying (oil fuel, fresh water, seawater, etc.), where it came from, and where it went to; what every valve was for (how to flood a compartment and how to pump it out); how a compartment is lit in an emergency; and what firefighting appliances are to hand, and how they work.

One other very important thing to know was the colour or number markings of the various valves, doors and hatches. X and Y doors were most important. Permission had to be obtained from the DCHS before an X door was opened; a Y door could be opened for passage without permission, but had to be immediately re-closed and secured.

Ship knowledge was very important indeed.

We squatted around enjoying our 'feast'. The Petty Officer was trying to get some information from the turret. Alby Clarke was in his 'private corner', head buried in one of his dirty books.

Stripey glanced up, and shouted, "Switch that bleeding pump off, somebody – and let's get out of here. I'm dying for a fag," he added, with a grin.

"Not much chance of that, Stripey," said the Petty Officer as he replaced the receiver. "I'll put you in the picture – we are about to meet up with the Malta force. I reckon they are copping some stick – bridge says they can hear gunfire up ahead, so on your toes, lads!"

Alby held out one of his books to Gordon, who passed the charges to me for our hoist.

"I bet you would like to have a butcher's at this," he leered. "Remind you of home."

Gordon had got married just prior to coming out to the Med, and Alby was often baiting him, and making him embarrassed with his dirty remarks.

"I'm not interested in that rubbish," said Gordon.

"Little lily-white, are you?" sneered Alby. "You aren't going to tell me you don't know what it's all about. Here – have a look," he persisted. "Shows all the little games you and your missus get up to."

"Shut your bloody trap," said Stripey.

"I bet he left a bun in the oven when he came out here," muttered Alby.

Petty Officer Wilson intervened: "Cut it out, Clarke – or I might just forget for a minute that I'm a petty officer."

Alby ignored him, and said, "He ain't no different from the

rest of us – I bet the dirty little bleeder dipped his wick in Alex the other night."

Stripey got slowly to his feet, walked over to Alby and said, "That kid is just a shrimp; how about picking on somebody your own size – like me, for instance!"

"Mind your own bloody business," said Alby. "I wasn't talking to you."

"I'm talking to you, you shithouse," replied Stripey. He reached out, took hold of the front of Alby's overalls and said in an icy voice, "Listen to this, you bloody louse, and remember it. If there is just one more word from you concerning that kid, I'll butt you so bloody hard you'll never recognise your face in the mirror again. And when I've done that I'll knee you so bloody hard you'll never want to look at your missus, or any other party [girl], for as long as you bleeding live."

Alby went as white as a sheet.

Stripey slammed him up against the bulkhead and came back to us.

"I'll stuff those bleeding books down his throat one of these times," he muttered.

"Stand to, lads!" Petty Officer Wilson gave the order, and we were on our feet in an instant, and ready. "Start the hoists!"

We felt relieved in an odd kind of way when the action started again. The worrying and tension went, and we would find ourselves laughing and joking perhaps. It was ridiculous really – perhaps we were becoming 'bomb happy'.

A rumble of explosions was heard – not very close. High-level bombers (probably) had dropped a whole stick.

'Watch your balance now,' I thought a moment or two later. The deck was beginning to tilt and I could feel the ship was turning. 'It's going to be our turn now – brace yourself!'

A tremendous crash came, and the ship staggered. Was it a single bomb, or had we been hit by a torpedo? The question was in all our minds, I imagine! There was no way of knowing down there what was happening. Our hoists were still clattering away, but that didn't tell us anything really. We could be on fire, or the sea could be rushing in through some torn plates. I hoped we were not going to roll over – behind the bulkhead at the after end of our magazine was another crew just like ours, and next to them a third crew – 'B' and 'Q' magazines. At the after end of the ship were the magazines of 'X' and 'Y' turrets. If the ship were to go over, we would all have had our chips – no question about that.

They Received a Communal Burial at Sea –
All sixty or So – Snug in Their Steel Boxes.

The ship seemed to be on an even keel still, so hopefully we were all right.

Seven more hammer blows followed at short intervals. Each one felt like a blow on the head, and sent our nerves jangling.

Dive-bombers! Stukas – that's what they were. They made an awful screaming noise when they came down – some of them had sirens fitted to their wings to increase the effect. They scared the living daylights out of us. When it seemed they must crash on to the ship, they would release their bomb, and pull out of the dive and away. All we could do then was to hope that the Captain, helmsman and telegraph men had 'got it right'.

There was another massive explosion alongside.

'How much can those hull plates stand?' I wondered.

That steel was not very thick. If it were to split, and the sea came pouring in, what would happen? It didn't bear thinking about. One thing was certain: they wouldn't risk opening the hatch to let us out – that could endanger the whole ship.

"We are getting mighty short of ammo," Gordon shouted in my ear.

I wasn't a bit surprised to hear that – it seemed as though I had pushed hundreds of charges into the hoist.

'We must not run out,' I thought. 'We have got the return journey to make yet. Maybe they won't bother us on the way back, knowing that the ships we are escorting are empty ones. Stupid idiot!' I told myself. 'You should know from previous trips that that fact won't stop them! How much longer have we got to be down here? My arms feel like lead weights, and my head is splitting – I wish those hoists would stop their racket. In charge, slam the door, then the reset – I reckon I could do it in my sleep. I wonder how the lads up in the turret are getting on.' One of my messmates was the shell loader on the R/H gun. 'I don't envy his job,' I thought (those shells weighed eighty pounds). 'On second thoughts, though, it wouldn't be too bad. The guns will be up to eighty or ninety degrees elevation, which means he will be dropping the shells down on to the loading tray, rather than lifting them up. I wonder if our turret, or any of the other turrets, have destroyed any of our attackers.'

It's a very chancy business, naval anti-aircraft gunnery – trying to shoot a fast-moving speck out of the sky when the guns themselves are moving in several different directions at the same time. The ship could be rolling and pitching as well as moving forward.

I imagine the gun turret gave the designers some headaches. In that limited space were the mountings and breeches of from two to four guns (their loading gear, in the case of battleships, had to handle shells of one ton in weight), as well as sights, ammunition supply, firefighting equipment, communications and, of course, the crew to work it all. This great mass of machinery had to be so balanced that it could be trained round to point accurately at a target, irrespective of what the ship itself was doing. When we consider that a sixteen-inch turret could weigh up to 1,500 tons, the mind begins to boggle. The turret structure had to be continued down into the magazine itself, of course, for the ammunition supply, and this had to be safe from a flash, in the event of an explosion in the turret.

'I hope we don't get a flash down here, but I don't suppose we would know anything about it. If the magazine went up we'd be instantly vaporised, I should think. No need to waste time looking for bits to bung.'

They Vanished at Sea Without Trace.

Several more explosions followed at short intervals. Then there was a bit of a lull, and we stood down.

I glanced around at the other faces – absolutely whacked, they looked, physically exhausted, heads numb from the explosions and the racket of the hoists, and all no doubt with the dumb acceptance that we would never escape with our lives. If not the next attack, or the one after that, maybe it would happen on the next trip. We came to accept it, to live with it, and not to worry.

Stripey's simple logic summed it up: "What's the point of worrying – it ain't going to change anything, is it?"

I can picture him still in my mind's eye – rolling shells into the hoist, a fierce grin on his face.

The Mediterranean Fleet had lost a lot of ships, and many hundreds of men. If only more air cover had been provided for us! What a difference it could have made!

I looked at my helper, Gordon. He was slumped in a corner, reading some of his wife's letters. At every opportunity, they came out of his pocket. Nineteen years old, like myself, Gordon had got married just before the ship left for the Eastern Mediterranean station.

'He must be going through hell,' I thought; 'and that poor girl of his – all the time, no doubt, wondering if he will ever come home again.'

I was glad I was not in the same situation. It must have been awful for all the wives, mothers and girlfriends waiting at home.

Home – it all seemed so far away and long ago now, but in actual fact it was only a few months since I had left.

I wondered what my old workmates were doing now. There were a few quite odd characters on the farm. Old Sam Swann, the foreman, came to mind. A tall scarecrow of a man, he stuttered a bit – I never knew where to look when he was talking to me! We boys used to copy him – not so he heard us, though. He was quite a reasonable old chap really; he got on all right with all the men. He would give us all our orders for the day, and leave us to get on with it. Often we wouldn't see any more of him. Old Sam was not a bit overawed by the boss, in spite of his loud voice and pompous manner, and would often give him back more than he bargained for.

An amusing incident came to mind, and I laughed aloud.

Stripey looked at me and said, "What do you find so bleeding funny, then?"

"I will tell you," I said. I explained briefly the sort of chap old Sam was, then what I was laughing at. "We were getting a bit behind with the harvest one time – at least the boss thought we were. Anyway he decided he would come and give us a hand himself, to 'shock' a field of barley.

"'He won't stick this long,' muttered one of the men, 'not when he's got a few of these thistles in his hands!'

"We were working down the field, towards the road, and presently I noticed old Sam standing in a gap in the hedge, watching us. A minute or two later, the boss spotted him.

"'Look at that lazy bugger standing there – time he lent a hand.' When we got a bit closer, he called out, 'How about lending the men a hand, Swann? You don't do a bloody stroke around here!'

"Back came Sam's reply: 'It's a p-p-poor old farm what can't s-s-support one lazy b-b-bugger!'"

It seemed to amuse Stripey and the others.

"Tell us some more, Matt," said one of the lads. "We can do with something to laugh at."

"All right," I said. "We were 'muck-carting' one morning, and it turned out quite funny. We were clearing out the horse yard, which was just the other side of the fence from the farmhouse. We had hardly got started when Mr Newman stuck his head out of the bedroom window.

"'The men were late getting started this morning, Swann!' he shouted.

"Old Sam looked up and stuttered, 'W-w-want some b-b-bricks and m-m-mortar up there!'

"'What the devil are you talking about, Swann?' asked the boss.

"'B-b-bricking up – s-s-see too much!'"

There was more laughter this time – I noticed the Petty Officer joined in.

"Any more stories?" asked someone.

"I think it is somebody else's turn now," I replied. "How about you, Stripey?" I asked. "I bet you could tell us a few tales."

He looked around at us all, grinned and said, "Well now, there was this party in Colombo!"

There followed a chorus of groans.

"Oh no – not that again!"

"I will tell you one more story," I said. "There was an old boy worked on the farm on a casual basis. Arty Gates was his name – Artful Arty we called him – the biggest liar and poacher in the neighbourhood. The stories he told us boys sometimes were too ridiculous for words. Anyway, on one particular occasion we were muck-spreading on one of the fields, and Arty began boasting about how good he was with his catapult. We all had catapults in our pockets in those days, and we were always on the lookout for nice round little stones, for ammunition. We also had a special pair of pliers for making lead balls," I added. "Anyway, Arty was boasting about how good he was.

"'I can knock a sparrow off the top of a barn roof – or a matchbox off a fence at twenty-five yards!'

"'Pull the other one, Arty,' said one of the men. 'You must think we are a lot of bloody idiots.'

"'That's a fact,' replied Arty. 'I can do it ten times out of ten – standing edgeways on,' he added.

"'You're sure you don't mean a matchstick?' asked Ned Neason.

"'That's a fact, I'm telling you – God strike me down if I tell a lie,' said Arty solemnly.

"'I shouldn't tempt Him if I were you, Arty boy,' replied Ned.

"'You can laugh,' said Arty. 'I'll tell you lot something now: I have knocked hundreds of pheasants out of trees, and there wasn't a mark on any one of them – except where my stone struck them on the head! I have got a special leather belt at home,' he went on. 'I sewed hooks all the way round it, and I can go out in the woods any night and have a pheasant hanging on every one by the time I get home!'

21

"'I reckon he is a bit touched in the head,' said one of the men, 'else he reckons all of us are.'

"I don't think Arty heard that, because he started off on another tale: 'That head keeper riled me the other night,' he said. 'He stopped me on the way home, and said, "Just a minute, Gates – I want a word with you. You were after my birds again last night, you old sod you." Blast! That wholly riled me, because I hadn't been out anywhere that night so as soon as he was out of sight, I said to myself, "Right, Mr Head Keeper, you are going to pay for that now." So in the woods I went, and got half a dozen!'"

Everyone in the magazine was laughing now.

"He must have been quite a character," said Petty Officer Wilson. "Had he got any family?"

"I never heard any mentioned at any time," I replied. "Arty lived in an old shack on a bit of waste ground in a nearby village. They gave him a job at one time with the gamekeeper – killing deer. Thought it the best way of keeping an eye on him, perhaps."

"Any more stories about him, Matt?" asked someone.

"I will tell you one more," I replied. I explained about an old muzzle-loading gun we used on the farm, for bird-scaring. "Arty was with us one day when the subject was brought up.

"'I had an old blunderbuss like that once,' he said. 'I remember one afternoon I loaded it with half a handful of small nails and went looking for something to shoot at. Well, there didn't seem to be any game about, but when I got nearly back home a flock of starlings came and settled in an old dead tree. "Right," I said. "I'll blast you lot." Well, I upped with the old gun, and let drive, and, do you know, those nails pinned about twenty of those starlings to the branches. If you go there and look, you will still see the remains of them – and that was thirty years ago!'"

That brought the house down! I think it did us all good.

Another series of attacks took place before we finally secured and fell out. We had been down there for fifteen hours.

CHAPTER 2

EARLY DAYS

My story really begins in the spring of 1940. When the war started I decided I would volunteer for the navy when I was eighteen. My brother Arthur, who was about a year and a half older than me, had joined the RAF, whilst my eldest brother, Fred, who was married, decided he would wait and register with his age group, and see what happened. Agriculture was a reserved occupation, and we all worked on a large farm near Newmarket, where in fact we had been born.

Anyway, Arthur and I volunteered and were accepted, whilst Fred and several of the other chaps about the same age remained on the farm throughout the war.

A few days after my eighteenth birthday I told my parents I was going to Cambridge to the recruiting office. My mother didn't say very much. She had lost her only brother in the First World War – perhaps she was remembering. He had been eighteen years old also. Apparently, he had received just five weeks' training before he was shipped over to France. He was dead within a fortnight.

Father was a bit surprised at my preference for the navy, I think. He had been an army regular, and was at Mons with the 5th Cavalry.

I told the farmer of my intention and asked for the morning off.

He agreed and said, "That's the spirit, boy. Get behind a bloody great gun and knock the hell out of somebody!"

So I took the train to Cambridge, and went down to the recruiting office. I was ushered into the office of a captain, Royal Marines, and said I wanted to join the navy for twelve years.

"Sorry, lad," he replied, "we are not recruiting for the regular service while the war is on, but you can certainly enlist for the duration; then re-enlist when it is over, should you still want to."

He took down a few particulars, and told me to report back on the following Monday for a medical, etc. This I did, and I seemed to be fit enough in all respects.

An amusing incident occurred while I was there. Several chaps had reported for their medicals, and one in particular was causing a bit of a problem. He had been drinking, apparently, and the Doctor was saying, "I'm afraid we are going to have to fit you in another time – I cannot examine you in the condition you are in."

"You had better try, Doc," was the reply, "because if I have to come again, I shall be a bloody sight worse."

I signed on the dotted line, and the recruiting officer told me I would be hearing from them in due course.

"It might be a few weeks, or a few months. It all depends on the position at the training establishment."

It was, in fact, six months. I had begun to think they had forgotten all about me.

It was about this time my brother Arthur went off to the RAF. As far as I remember, he did his basic training at Cardington in Bedfordshire, then went to a Spitfire squadron at Hawkinge.

Meanwhile, things were happening at home. Newmarket Rowley Mile racecourse had been turned into an airfield, and in the early months of the war we used to watch the aeroplanes taking off in the evening, and would sometimes hear them returning in the early hours of the morning.

"I hope they've all got back," my mother would say.

A section of the Devil's Dyke had been lowered by several feet to help their take-off.

We were gradually becoming conditioned to the need for food rationing and a total blackout. More and more people were to be seen in uniform.

Work on the farm went on much as usual, although plans were put into effect to increase food production. Several acres of meadows were ploughed up, and also some stretches of rough grassland.

The war news seemed more depressing every day: the collapse of the French, the rout of our own army and the evacuation from Dunkirk, the increasing air attacks on the country, and the threat of invasion. Roadblocks were set up at strategic points, the Home Guard was formed, all signposts were removed, and private firearms of all descriptions were made ready. Those that didn't have a gun selected a suitable club, hook or pitchfork!

How we would fare against the highly trained and well-equipped professional German Army didn't bear thinking about. There was no lack of spirit or determination, however, and the Home Guard did become a very efficient force. One great thing the war did was to make people realise how dependent we all were on one another.

One evening we had a practice session on knocking out enemy tanks. An old armoured car, probably dating from the First World War, was towed to the farm and parked in the corner of a field, and we threw bottles of petrol and phosphorous at it – great fun, we younger lads thought, but that phosphorous was nasty stuff!

Rumour had it that an invasion attempt had already been made, but had been smashed at sea. However, I believe the official history of the war discounts this. One 'German invasion' exercise had been attacked by some of our aircraft, and several landing craft and barges had been sunk. This, no doubt, had given rise to the rumour.

"They won't get here," Father said. "The navy will see to that!"

Probably the navy would have scotched any seaborne attempt; but if the Germans had carried out mass landings of airborne troops, I shudder to think what might have happened.

There was some air activity in our district about this time, and one attack resulted in the sad death of one of our workmates –

old Jimmy Claydon, a small scarecrow of a man, not very intelligent and well past retiring age. We were all guilty, at times, of teasing and making fun of him. Some of the men would go too far sometimes, and the poor old chap would get in a terrible state.

He was employed on the farm as an odd-job man, doing such things as cutting down beds of thistles and nettles on the meadows, clearing up odd corners, and bird-scaring in the wintertime.

Mr Newman, the farmer, who was a surly and impatient man at the best of times, had very little time for poor old Jimmy. I recall a heated discussion I overheard one morning. It wasn't really a discussion – Mr Newman did all the talking, shouting.

Old Jimmy's vocabulary was very limited indeed. He answered with the word 'yes' to everything the boss said to him. He didn't actually say 'yes' – 'ess' was Jimmy's word.

Mr Newman, losing what little patience he had, was trying to make old Jimmy understand what he wanted him to do – which fields he wanted him to keep the birds off (the Sidehill, the Top Heath, and so on) and which fields he need not bother about.

Poor old Jimmy answered 'ess' to everything, and Mr Newman, more purple than ever now, finally shouted at him, "Damn you, Claydon – go where you bloody well like!"

"Ess," replied Jimmy.

It was only by a miracle he survived his bird-scaring days. An ancient blunderbuss was the weapon used for bird-scaring, and old Jimmy was often seen peering down the barrel because he couldn't remember whether he had loaded it or not. The gun was in a very dangerous condition – barrel rusty and pitted, stock bound up with wire, and the hammer-and-trigger mechanism very worn. It was very risky indeed to leave it at half- or full-cock, but still one or two of us young lads and old Jimmy would bang it off to scare the birds.

Old Jimmy died one evening during the early part of the harvest. It was nearly leaving-off time, while we were clearing up loose straw around the elevator in the stackyard.

We were talking about the war and the air raids when one of the men said something about "That swine Hitler."

Old Jimmy brandished his fork and said, "I'll stick 'un!"

Half an hour or so later he was dead. A lone Heinkel III dropped a stick of bombs close by the house where Jimmy lodged, and the first of them fell on the outhouse. He had gone in there for something only a minute or so before, we heard later.

No trace of him was found.

We all had a lucky escape a week or two later. We were carting wheat at the time, and as I was pitching a sheaf up to one of the men loading the wagon I spotted a plane coming towards us from an easterly direction.

I called to the chap above me: "Charlie, that plane looks like a Dornier 215 to me."

He grinned down at me and replied, "You boys – every plane you see is a bloody Jerry!"

I kept my eyes on it, and when it was almost directly overhead I saw the bombs beginning to fall.

"Charlie!" I shouted, and pointed up to the sky.

In less time than it takes to tell, he was on the ground beside me. Then he vanished. I think he must have dived head first into the nearest corn shock!

The bombs were going to drift beyond us, I decided. I went to the horse's head and grabbed hold of the bridle. After a few seconds the explosions came – quite loud, but not as loud as I thought they might have been. The horse was not unduly alarmed.

I turned around and saw a great cloud of smoke and dust in the next field, and felt very fearful for my mother as our house was just over there. I began to run in that direction, and was relieved to see the house was still intact as the dust began to clear.

Mother was a bit shaken up, but otherwise all right, although the first pair of bombs had fallen only about seventy yards away. There were eighteen craters across the field, and one pair of the bombs had straddled a tractor-drawn binder. Amazingly, no one was hurt. Four incendiaries had fallen near when Charlie and I were working, and we smothered these with soil.

We wondered afterwards what the target had been – surely not a harvest field? Somebody told us later the craters were directly in line with the runway on the Rowley Mile airfield. If they had been aiming for that, it was not a very good effort. They had fallen over a mile short.

The men who were stacking the wheat we had been carting had seen the bombs falling also, and had come down from the stack to take cover. My brother Fred said one of his mates had overtaken him coming down the ladder!

Much of the work on farms in those days was hard physically, the hours long and pay low, but the work was much more varied and interesting than it is today. It is much more satisfying to do a job with your own hands, rather than operating a machine to do it for you.

We were getting on well with the harvest – most of the fields had been cleared. Soon it would be time for the mangold crop to be lifted and clamped, then the sugar beet after that. This was one of the more unpleasant jobs, especially if we had rainy weather.

The beet were lifted by a special plough, but had to be 'knocked and topped' by hand. It was not very pleasant either if there had been a frost overnight.

Later on, the horse and stack yards would be cleared out, and the muck carted out to the fields to be spread – by hand – ready for ploughing. Three, and sometimes four, double ploughs, each drawn by three horses, would be at work on the same field. There was also a three-furrow plough, drawn by an International tractor. I didn't envy the driver's job – no centrally heated cabs in those days! More than once I saw him jump off the tractor and walk behind the plough, slapping his arms across his chest to try to get his circulation going again, then dash up ahead and hop back on.

A great thrill for me as a young lad was when the steam-plough tackle came. Once I was permitted to stand up on one of the engines alongside the driver! I watched fascinated as the seven-furrow plough got ever nearer, once or twice with some alarm when I thought it was going to crash into us; then the driver would bring it to a halt, perhaps only inches from the engine. They would work till nearly midnight sometimes, giving whistle signals to each other.

There were no slack periods on farms in those days – plenty to do all the year round. In the winter there would be all the corn stacks to be threshed; also several weeks' work of hedging and ditching. In bad weather there would be machinery maintenance, and such things as jacking all the wagons and carts up, removing the wheels and greasing the axles and undercarriages. Some of the wheels would need to be re-tyred also.

Many days would be spent in the barns, dressing, weighing and sacking up the corn; many more in the stable harness room, polishing up the brasses and oiling the leather, often by the light of a hurricane lantern! The farmhouse had its own little power plant, but there was no power in the outbuildings – no heating either.

I spent two winters as a shepherd's boy. Pretty arduous work this, especially when it was very cold. I had to set fresh folds and pull up the old ones – rolling up wire netting in the snow. More than once I could have cried with finger ache. How the old shepherd managed to use that steel fold drift for making holes for the stakes I will never know. He never wore gloves, and the cracks on his hands were awful. It was most difficult making the holes, and when we had severe frosts the stakes would get frozen in. Every time I broke one off, trying to get them out, he would round on me and swear.

"Watch what you're doing, boy – there won't be a bloody stake long enough to use soon!"

He had quite a large flock – over 300 black-faced Suffolks. I'll swear he knew them all individually. "That old lop-eared one, boy," or "that old black-faced", and so on. They all looked the same to me! One job I hated was holding the little lambs while he burned their tails off and castrated them. How those poor little things bleated!

Flocks of sheep and shepherds on this farm had won many prizes at the big shows in earlier years. The walls of a compartment in one of the buildings bore testimony in the form of row upon row of certificates – first, second and third prizes, highly commended, etc. There were hundreds of them, some barely legible.

Springtime working on the farm was quite pleasant, walking up and down the field at a leisurely pace harrowing, rolling and drilling, with a team of two or three horses. It was peaceful and quiet – just the sound of the implement going through the soil, and the jingling of the harness and the birdsong. I don't think I would like to be a present-day farm worker.

How different the countryside looked in those days! No sprays or weedkillers were used, and it was quite an education to us children to see how many different kinds of wild flowers we could find. One of the meadows behind our house was a blaze of colour in the springtime – great beds of buttercups, daisies, cowslips, and various other flowers. The twenty or so horses – mainly Suffolks – would be turned out there after having their feed, together with the cows. It was a lovely sight.

When the springtime work was completed, it would be time for haymaking, and then on to the harvest again.

I spent two winters as 'bird-scaring boy'. I quite liked this job – it gave me a feeling of independence, of being my own boss, so to speak! Wandering from field to field on various parts of the farm, banging the old blunderbuss off now and again, I felt released and free.

In very cold weather, I would light a fire at a nice sheltered spot in a spinney, or on the edge of a wood, leave my docky bag there, and every now and again, on my rounds, I would stoke it up and have a little warm.

We had a half-hour breakfast break in those days, and I would toast my bacon sandwiches, pies, etc. Great fun! But I had to watch out for the boss on his old mare. I didn't want him finding a flock of pigeons on his kale!

A very odd and amusing incident occurred one morning. It was quite early – barely light in fact – and quite foggy. I was walking over a field where there were a lot of mole runs when something moving a short distance ahead attracted my attention.

I walked on a few yards, but there was nothing to be seen.

'I must have imagined it,' I thought. 'Maybe it's the fog playing tricks.'

But no – there it was again, a little way off to the right this time. Something on the ground – it appeared to be quite long – was moving quickly. Then it vanished again.

'Whatever is it?' I wondered. 'It isn't a snake. There aren't any around here.'

I was completely mystified. Standing quite still, I scanned the ground all around me; then suddenly something came out of a mole run, about four feet away.

It was, in fact, a whole family of weasels. Round and round they went, then vanished, to reappear a few yards away. It was getting a bit brighter by now, and I watched them for several minutes as they moved further and further away. Perhaps they were playing follow-the-leader!

The old blunderbuss we used was a pretty-fearsome close-range weapon when charged with small tin tacks, or air-gun pellets. Sitting rabbits or pheasants were the targets, and sometimes we would charge the gun with a solid lead ball for targets at a longer range!

We carried an old cocoa tin full of gunpowder in one pocket, and a tin of percussion caps and small wads of newspaper in the other. It beggars belief, thinking about it now. Fourteen- and fifteen-year-old boys walking around with tins of gunpowder in their pockets!

The bowl of an old briar pipe was used to measure the correct amount of powder, and the old foreman would give us strict instructions to stick to that amount.

"Half a pipeful, boy – and no more!"

We stuck to that at first, then thought we would experiment – three-quarters of a pipeful, a full pipe, and more. It was a wonder we never had a serious (or even fatal) accident, the stupid things we did.

I remember one incident in particular. I had already loaded the gun with powder and paper and wondered what I could charge it with. Fishing around in my pockets, I came across a bicycle cotter pin – the bolt that held the pedal crank on.

'Looks about the right size,' I thought, and I dropped it down the barrel.

I carried on walking, looking for something to shoot at, but a little nagging doubt had crept into my mind.

'Maybe it's not a good idea after all,' I thought. 'It might burst the barrel, or even blow my hand off. I don't think I will risk it.'

Tilting the barrel down, I tried to shake the cotter pin out, but it was wedged. Too late I remembered the barrel tapered down towards the breech.

'Hell!' I thought. 'Now I am in a fix. I daren't tell the foreman – I will have to fire it!'

A little distance ahead was an outlying bullock yard.

'I ought to find a target here,' I thought.

Presently a blackbird flew by and settled on top of the fence.

'This is it,' I thought.

I raised the gun above my head, then threw my arm down in the general direction of the target and pulled the trigger.

I didn't hit the blackbird, but the cotter pin went clean through the fence. I was fifteen at the time.

Another nasty incident comes to mind, when I almost shot myself in the foot. As I mentioned earlier, the hammer-and-trigger mechanism was very worn and liable to slip. The foreman had warned us never to walk around with the gun on half- or full-cock. I did, this particular morning, and a lead ball went about four inches into the soil quite close to my feet!

I recall my father telling me that the district was reckoned to be the best partridge ground in the whole country. How true that was I don't know, but I can well believe it. Covey after covey I would put up – fifteen to eighteen birds in some of them. In the autumn, the gamekeeper would stick lots of thorn bushes over the stubbles to foil the poachers with their nets.

One autumn I had a good haul of partridges, involving no effort on my part – they were lying there just waiting to be picked up. One of the fields on my beat at this particular time was alongside the railway embankment, and on foggy mornings sometimes coveys of birds flying over the railway would hit the telephone wires, and some would be killed. Naturally, I didn't leave them lying there!

One morning, I picked six birds up, and was walking along to my hiding place when the dim shape of a figure appeared ahead in the mist.

'That looks like Tom Pearman, the head gamekeeper,' I thought, and I quickly popped my bag behind a clump of bushes I was passing.

I had pretty sharp eyes in those days, and I hoped I had seen him before he spotted me, and what I was carrying.

We met and he said, "Morning, boy."

"Morning, Mr Pearman," I replied, crossing my fingers.

He was a hard, stern man, and we boys were more than a little scared of him.

"Nasty morning, boy."

"Yes, Mr Pearman."

'I hope that retriever bitch of his don't scent those birds,' I thought.

Fortunately, she didn't.

"Did you see any gyppos by the covey gate, boy?"

"No, Mr Pearman, I didn't come through there. I crossed the road further up."

"All right, boy, there was a trike there when I came along, and I gave them half an hour to move on. If they are still there when I get back, then over goes the cart!"

"You wouldn't do that, Mr Pearman?"

"I would, boy, and I will."

Legally, he could do nothing about it useless they were on private property, but I don't think that would have deterred him.

I came to know the families of Gypsies a few years later, and I decided that on the whole they were pretty harmless. All they asked was to be allowed to live the life they chose, and a place to park their van at night. They didn't leave a mess when they moved on either – the dealer/traveller types were the untidy ones.

George and Mag Allgood were simple and uncomplicated folk.

They had three fine children at the time I knew them. Sarah was about eight years old, a pretty little thing, but very shy. It was some time before she would even speak to me. Levi was a year or two younger than Sarah, and a friendly little lad. Neither child could read or write. They also had a baby of about eighteen months old.

They used some shocking language – children as well as parents – but after a while I realised it was their usual way of talking to one another. I remember one Sunday in particular. I hadn't known them very long, and we were having dinner (Mag made some very tasty stews in the pot) when George asked Sarah to get him the salt from the van. She didn't take a bit of notice and carried on eating her dinner.

"Sarah," said George, in a slightly raised voice, "I asked you to get me the salt!"

Little Sarah looked at him, and without batting an eyelid, said, "You get the - - - - - - yourself, you old - - - - you. You've got two legs, haven't you!"

'Hell!' I thought. 'That's a bit strong from an eight-year-old.'

I caught George's eye, and he gave a little lopsided grin. Mag pretended to look shocked.

George and Mag were well provided for, transport-wise. They had a smart little bow-top van and a flat trolley.

I spent several weekends one summer painting all the pretty bits on their bow-top. George had remarked a couple of times it needed doing.

"You won't get better weather than now," I replied the second time.

"Huh," said Mag. "That old - - - - couldn't do it – his hand is too - - - - - - - shaky!"

George taught me how to make chrysanthemums or asters from privet wood. He would skin the bark off a piece about finger-thick; then, with a very sharp knife, he would shave it down very thinly all round, to a length of about three inches. The shavings would all curl back on one another. Round and round he went until he came almost to the centre; then he'd snap the piece off. I soon learned that the trick was to draw the wood against the knife blade, and not the other way around.

After making a hole in the centre with an awl, Mag would insert a suitable stem with green leaves, and when the flowers had been dyed different colours they looked almost like the natural thing.

The other Gypsy family I saw from time to time over a period of several years were the Parkers. I learned a few things from them also.

Old Dan Parker showed me how to make clothes pegs – he was an artist at this, and so quick. Mrs Parker's speciality was making cyclamen flowers from wax.

Their daughter Amy showed me how to make roses from coloured crêpe papers. She would cut a strip about three inches wide and eighteen inches long, double it end to end, then double it again, then cut quite a pronounced wavy pattern along one side. Then, lying the paper over the palm of her hand, she would stretch out each bulge with the handle of a tablespoon, which caused it to curl. A few quick twists, and there was a perfect rose, to be wired to a suitable stem. Amy could make full-blown roses, roses half out and roses in the bud stage – all most realistic.

I will always associate the Parker family with the Slim Whitman record 'China Doll'. Amy had an old wind-up gramophone, and she played that record over and over again. It became so badly worn that I decided one day when in town to buy her a replacement. Amy was so pleased. I think it made her day.

Tom Pearman, the head gamekeeper, was a bit of a mystery man. It was rumoured that he had killed a man in his younger days. Two chaps he had caught poaching, and who had been fined, were out for revenge, and apparently they lay in wait for him one night.

This is the tale I got from one of the older men on the farm: "Tom told me himself. He said, 'I saw them waiting, and reversed my stick, which had a heavy knob on the end. The first one came at me, and I downed him, and then the other.' The next morning, one of them was found lying there dead."

We never heard any mention of a Mrs Pearman. Tom lived with his daughter and her husband, and their daughter. The latter was the same age as me – we sort of grew up together. Both mother and daughter were black-haired, swarthy, and very superstitious. I often wondered where they came from.

The Battle of Britain was in full swing at this time, and we heard many aircraft going over in the night sometimes. The air-raid sirens went off frequently, and one night two bombs, probably dropped at random, fell not far from our house. One of them left a mound of soil, like a giant molehill. It must have been a dud, we thought, but I don't remember what happened about it – if anything.

One night we stood in our garden, watching the searchlights probing back and forth, and we could hear aircraft engines. Presently one of the beams found their target, and others quickly followed. An aeroplane glowed as a white cross in the brilliance. A few seconds later we saw the sparkle of gunfire, a short distance behind it, and it immediately began to spiral down. We all cheered.

In early October my call-up came at last. I was to report to HMS *Ganges* at Shotley, near Ipswich, on the following Monday.

CHAPTER 3

HMS *GANGES*

There was a large crowd of men milling about on Ipswich Station, and more on the road outside. Many were about my own age; some were several years older. I felt that I was among a crowd of foreigners. Among the Scots and North Country accents there didn't appear to be any local ones at all.

A petty officer, my first glimpse of authority, was trying, with some difficulty, to shepherd us across the road to a fleet of buses.

New intakes of men went to *Ganges* annexe, across the road from the main barracks. Here we were medically inspected and kitted up, etc. We filled out various forms and had photographs taken for our pay books. Then we were given a chat by the padre, and a lecture by the Doctor.

What a business that kitting-up and uniform-fitting was! There seemed to be one special method only of getting the jumper on and off, but most of us soon got the hang of it, and after a few days I felt quite comfortable in my uniform.

All our kit had to be marked with our names, and we were shown how to lay it out for inspection. Another thing we learned in that first day or two was how to assemble, sling and lash up a hammock. We would be needing them at sea, but here we slept in beds.

The living quarters were spotlessly clean and spacious, the food good and plentiful. We were invited to get second helpings, if we wanted.

We were taught how to salute, and how to 'off caps' and 'on caps'. Pretty tricky manoeuvres these, we found! At the order 'off caps', the right hand had to move up smartly to the left side of the head, grasp the edge of the hat with thumb and forefinger, remove it and take it down in one movement behind the back. At the order 'on caps', the movement was reversed, and we hoped we would get it back on our head somehow! At the order 'stand at ease – stand easy', we could adjust it, of course.

The instructors were very patient and helpful, answering our many questions and showing us how to do things.

'Great life this!' we thought.

We were deluding ourselves of course, as we were to soon find out. The final talk given to us by the annexe commander made us think a bit.

"We have let you off lightly here," he said. "You will find it very different over the road. Discipline is much more strict, but just and fair. Don't let it worry you – just do your best. Good luck to you all."

Our kitbags and hammocks had been taken over to the main barracks for us, and now we ourselves marched over.

'What will it be like?' we wondered.

Our two instructors introduced themselves: Chief Gunner's Mate Taylor, and Chief Petty Officer Wallace.

The former took over now: "It will be my job to teach you how to march, left turn, right turn and about turn. Then, as soon as you have sorted your left and right feet out, we will have a go at some rifle drill. It will be essential then to know which are your left and right shoulders. The most important thing to remember is when I shout, you jump to it – quick! Chief Petty Officer Wallace will be your seamanship instructor. He will teach you all you need to know about knots and splices, rigging, boats, flags and signals – all the things a jolly Jack tar needs to know. There will be other interesting things to do when you get to sea, such as scrubbing down decks, painting the mast and the ship's side, etc."

I thought I detected a faint smile on Chief Petty Officer Wallace's face, but it was gone in an instant.

The Chief Gunner's Mate was off again: "Now pay attention. You have become part of the Royal Navy, that splendid service with all its great traditions. You will find the going pretty hard at times; discipline is very strict, but fair. Co-operate, behave yourselves, and you will get on well in the splendid service, and we will be like fathers to you. On the other hand, if you should decide you don't want to co-operate and accept things as they are, you will quickly get yourselves disliked. And if you should decide to be really awkward, you will very soon find the splendid service can be a - - - - - - - sight more awkward than ever you can!"

There was dead silence. We all knew, by the tone of his voice, he wasn't kidding. His gaze moved from face to face.

"We have got to try to teach you in ten weeks what takes one year in peacetime. What a hopeless-looking lot! God help us!"

'What have I let myself in for?' I wondered.

I had heard what HMS *Ganges* was like from two local chaps who had joined as boy seamen. Both were several years older than I was, and navy regulars. I used to see one of them quite often when he was on leave, as he would call to see his uncle, who was a shepherd on the farm.

"*Ganges* is hell on earth," he told me. "You don't get a minute's peace – you have to run everywhere, and you are shouted at from morning to night."

I think every boy who was there longed for the day when the course was finished.

We were standing in the long covered way, which had accommodation blocks (or 'messes', as the navy called them) on either side.

Chief Petty Officer Wallace took over now: "Right then, lads, we will go into the mess – you can stow your gear in the racks provided and select a bed. Don't be too fussy which one – they are all the same. Squad, 'shun! Right turn. By the left, quick march! Squad, halt! We will try a different approach.

Squad, 'shun! In a heap, towards that door, turn. By the left – or right – walk!"

We spent the remainder of the first day studying barrack routine and standing orders, and we were taken on a quick tour of the barracks.

The second day, we were divided into two sections. While half of us were in the classrooms, the others would be on the parade ground or in the gymnasium. Later there were also boat instructions, and sessions in the six-inch-gun battery and swimming pool.

My first session in the pool was a bit alarming, to put it mildly. Briefly, the fifteen or so non-swimmers in my class were piped to report to the pool one morning, ordered to strip off – completely – and were then pushed into the pool, one after another. I was a bit slow undressing, apparently, because I found myself well up towards the deep end.

"A deep breath, lad. Hold it. In you go!"

I had never been in really deep water before, and I panicked immediately. They had to fish me out, together with four or five others.

"Sorry about our crude methods," said the physical-training instructor, "but there's no time to mess about. Learn if you can, lads, before you go – it's in your own interest."

I thoroughly enjoyed the physical-training sessions, and climbing up over the huge mast. It dominated the parade ground, and all the lads were expected to climb it, but at least we were not helped on by a knotted rope's end, as were the peacetime boy seamen. We had to climb up the rigging to the crow's nest, through the hole in the centre ('the lubber's hole') up to the upper yardarm, over it, and down the other side to the crow's nest again. Next, for some of the chaps, came the most worrying part. We were not permitted to come back down through the centre of the crow's nest, but had to clamber over the outside of it. We found ourselves clinging for dear life to an iron rod, desperately trying to get a foothold on the rigging beneath us. A huge safety net was stretched about seven feet above the ground, beneath the mast, and we heard lurid stories of men falling from the mast, bouncing off this, and right over the top of the nearest building!

I would have loved to have climbed to the top of the mast, but it was not permitted, although I did go up to the half-moon one day, which was way above the upper yard. As a child, and a young lad, I had spent countless hours climbing trees of all kinds, buildings and corn and straw stacks on the farm.

My young pal and I had one special climbing place. It was a row of large crab-apple trees behind our house, and we found we could clamber through sixteen trees before we came down to the ground again. Some of the intertwining branches were mighty thin, but we were both lightweights.

Our training progressed, and the day arrived for our first session at the six-inch-gun battery. A mighty hectic affair it turned out to be. We had been through the theory in the classroom – now for the real thing! Chief Gunner's Mate Taylor was in his element now. He divided us into two crews; and while one was put through the drill, the other watched. The various gun positions were manned – layer, trainer, breech-worker, sight-setter, etc. Spare hands were shell and cordite loaders, and ammunition suppliers. A few pretend rounds were fired, and then we all changed positions. The shells were wooden ones, and we kept running them up the breech until they fell out at the other end, whereupon spare hands retrieved them.

Chief Gunner's Mate Taylor stood there, legs braced wide apart, hands on hips, roaring out the orders: "PI gun, close up. Clear away. Load, load, load. Barrage firing – commence, commence, commence!"

There would be tremendous activity for a minute or two, and then the order "PI gun, cease firing. Check, check, check!"

"Look at old Taylor's face," said one of the lads alongside me. "I bet the old bastard thinks he's back at Jutland!"

'He could well have been there too,' I found myself thinking. 'He is the right kind of age.'

Little did I realise then that I would actually fire a six-inch gun at sea.

Practice boat-pulling in November and December was not very pleasant, dressed only in shorts and singlets – no gloves permitted.

We had some nasty moments on the .303 rifle range. Probably most of the chaps had never handled a firearm of any description, and it is unbelievable the muddles they got into.

"Pull that rifle tight in to your shoulder," the Chief Gunner's Mate would bellow. "We don't want the sickbay full of broken jaws!" Despite the warnings, some chaps suffered minor injuries.

Most of us found the course quite reasonable, I think, all things considered, but there are always a few non-triers and idiots around. Our instructor had us all weighed up, I think, and he soon sorted the skivers and smart alecs out. The instructors had a pretty demanding job to do, and I take my hat off to them.

We had a number of evening and weekend trips into Ipswich and across the water to Harwich. It was nice to get away for a few hours, and small parties of men would form up and strut around town, pretending they were real jolly Jack tars!

We were not fooling anyone but ourselves, however, as our brand-new nearly black collars, and hats perched on the side of our heads, were a dead giveaway.

I did not form any particular friendship at *Ganges*, but two of the lads did become really close mates. Laurel and Hardy, we called them, and there really was a striking resemblance. I was to see them again one day in Egypt, at the Fleet Club in Alexandria, still together on the same ship. It was not much of a ship really – one of those small lighters running supplies up to Tobruk after it was cut off. A very dangerous mission this, and a number of lighters were sunk and their crews killed. They called their little jetty in Alexandria Harbour 'the condemned cell'. I learned that Laurel and Hardy had actually shot down a Heinkel bomber with their single pom-pom. These two and one other lad were the only ones of my *Ganges* classmates I ever saw again. It was quite likely many of them lost their lives on the Malta convoys.

Our ten-week course was nearing its end, and we were frantically swotting up for our seamanship exams. There were so many things to remember: how to tie all the different knots (how many different whippings were used, long and short splices, back splices); the different markings on a hand lead line; boxing the compass; the difference between standing and running rigging; the rule of the road at sea; the different types of buoys and their markings; the contents of a boat box . . .

There seemed to be no end to the things we might be asked, but we were given some small consolation by Chief Petty Officer Wallace.

"One thing is sure," he said (with his tongue in his cheek, I suspect): "they won't be asking you about all of them."

We also worried about the parade-ground drill, and the passing-out parade.

One lad, throughout the course, had had the greatest difficulty fixing his bayonet securely. Often when we ordered arms his bayonet would clatter to the deck, and the Chief Gunner's Mate would go berserk.

"If that happens at the passing-out parade," he told Ordinary Seaman Jake one day, "I will personally use that bayonet for a very painful and humiliating purpose!"

He needn't have worried, as it turned out.

Several other classes passed out on the same day, and I think it must have been quite a spectacle with the band playing and all the lads marching. Chief Gunner's Mate Taylor's craggy face was beaming. I think he was really pleased with our performance.

We met our two instructors in the canteen that evening for a farewell drink, and as I shook hands with the Chief Gunner's Mate I noticed tears in his eyes.

Our different port divisions had been allocated – my own being HMS *Pembroke,* Chatham. Other lads were divided up between Portsmouth and Devonport. It depended mainly on what part of the country you came from. Kitbags and hammocks had been packed, and would be transported for us. All that remained now was to go through the drafting routine – medical, etc.

CHAPTER 4

CHATHAM BARRACKS

HMS *Pembroke* was a 'store frigate', as we called shore bases. It seemed absolute chaos inside that immense drill shed. A mountain of kitbags and hammocks, hundreds of men milling around, and chief petty officers roaring out orders – this was our introduction to HMS *Pembroke*.

Groups of men were sitting on the kitbags, or lounging around, looking about and wondering what had hit them. Gone was the relative calm and ordinariness of HMS *Ganges*; here it was all noise and confusion.

"What are you all hanging around for, then?" a voice bellowed. "You have been allocated your messes – now get off your arses, grab your kitbags and hammocks, and get cracking!"

'Grab my kitbag and hammock? It might be right at the bottom of that bloody great heap,' I thought.

"You are like a lot of old whores at a picnic," the voice went on. "On your feet, you lot!" – this to a group who were sitting chatting to one another. "Are you - - - - - - - well deaf? Chop-chop! Move your bleeding selves!"

I looked at the slip of paper I had been given. 'Nelson Block, Mess GC4', it said. It might just as well have been in a foreign language for all it meant to me. I didn't have a clue where Nelson Block was, or what it looked like. I felt a moment of panic – none of my old classmates were in sight, and I felt very alone. We had hoped we would be staying together, but of course there wasn't much chance of that happening.

"You are on your own now, Jack," I said. "Time to start standing on your own two feet."

"Right then, where are you for?" the voice of authority shouted in my ear. A hand came over my shoulder and grabbed my slip of paper. "Nelson, GC4 – over the parade ground, up the steps; block on your right. Get cracking!"

HMS *Ganges* was small compared with this barracks. The huge parade ground had a high terrace on one side, with four massive barrack blocks above. On the other side was the drill shed, and many other buildings of all kinds were spread over a large area.

I made myself known to the leading hand of the mess, when I found it, and he gave me a few tips: "Don't leave any gear or personal belongings lying around," he said, "or they might walk. Also, be here on time for meals, or you won't get any."

'This is going to be a pretty depressing place,' I thought. 'I hope I'm not here too long.'

The barracks was teeming with men. There must have been many hundreds. I didn't see any of my old classmates around – it was already as though they had never existed.

HMS *Pembroke* was a transit base. Men were coming and going all the time, and it gave me the feeling I was completely on my own; I didn't want to know anybody, and I didn't feel I could trust anybody. Discipline was very strict – much of it petty and needless, I thought.

One instance in particular comes to mind. I was walking down to the main gate one afternoon, going on evening shore leave, when whistles began blowing and the sentry at the gate started waving his arms and shouting in my direction.

'What's the matter with him?' I wondered. 'Is he trying to attract my attention? If so, for what reason? I am properly dressed – hat on square, collar straight – and I've got my gas mask. What else can there be?'

I carried on walking along the pavement, which bordered quite a wide road. Suddenly a messenger came dashing towards me.

"Whatever is the matter?" I asked.

"You – walking on that bleeding pavement," he replied. "They call it the Commodore's Walk. Only he is permitted to walk on there!"

'I don't believe what I'm hearing,' I thought: a wide pavement reserved for just one bloke, and all the other hundreds to use the road! How ridiculous can they get!'

I stepped into the road, and got a roasting when I cruised out through the main gate: "Don't you read barrack rules and regulations, you stupid sod?"

"Not that one apparently," I replied. "Have we got to walk in the road and risk getting knocked down by a truck?"

"Don't be bloody cheeky," was the reply, "or you'll be in the rattle [on a charge]. I don't make the rules – I'm just here to see that stupid bastards like you obey them!"

Needless to say, I was mightily relieved to get out, and as I walked along the road to town I thought, 'That could have been a bit dodgy. I could easily have been up on two or three charges: failing to read barrack rules and regulations, failing to comply with same and being insolent to a superior. They would very likely have thought of something else as well.

In some parts of the barracks you had to go 'at the double', and I remember one particular nasty little noticeboard in the drill shed that caught many blokes out.

One side said, 'Oilskins to Be Carried', and the other said, 'Negative Oilskins'. There existed a squad of chief petty officers, with whistles hanging around their necks, whose sole purpose in life seemed to be to pick up as many blokes as they could on some pretext or other. We came to call them the Gestapo, and *Pembroke* Barracks the Gaol.

The general daily routine was for all hands to muster in the drill shed, where we would be detailed off for all manner of jobs around the barracks and nearby dockyard. Parties of men would be sweeping up different areas, picking up litter, engaged on various painting operations, handling stores, etc.

Many men would be working in the dockyard each day, loading ships, painting ships, chipping paint off ships, ammunitioning or de-ammunitioning ships . . . It must have been an almighty headache for someone, keeping everybody occupied.

46

I was with a party one morning, detailed off for chipping paint off a submarine. The leading hand in charge of us marched us down to the dockyard paint store, after first collecting our station cards (barrack identity documents), and here we were issued with chipping harnesses and scrapers.

The submarine was in a dry dock, with wooden staging all around her.

"Spread yourselves out," the leading hand said, "and no sloping off."

"Not much chance of that," my neighbour said. "He has got our cards in his pocket."

It was a very boring job, and some of the chaps got chippings in their eyes.

After a while I said to my neighbour, "I'm getting fed up with this – let's have a break. Let's go and have a look inside her."

"Better ask someone first," he replied.

We spotted our Leading Seaman a few minutes later, and I called out to him to ask if it was all right.

"No," he snapped, "it bleeding well isn't. You are here to chip paint off the outside – not to go snouting about inside."

"Surly bastard!" said my neighbour.

On another occasion in the dockyard one morning it became quite hilarious, but also a bit alarming. A party of four of us had been detailed off to paint the dockyard commander's car. It was not actually his own car, but one he used for his duties. We collected paint, brushes and rags from the stores, and the leading seaman in charge of us said, "If I haven't been down to see you by the time they pipe 'cooks to the galley', take your gear back to the stores, and I will bring your cards down. OK?"

We started to work on the car (battleship grey) and 'stand easy' came and went. We were getting on very well until one of the lads began fooling around with his brush. Then I suppose we all got a bit carried away. We painted practically everything, inside and out – lamps, door handles, steering wheel, gear lever, dashboard and instruments. Nothing escaped! I suppose we eventually came to our senses, and walked around looking at our handiwork.

"Jesus Christ Almighty!" exclaimed one lad. "They will shoot us!"

"What a mess!" said another. "What's that killick [leading seaman] going to say when he sees it?"

"I reckon they will be piping 'cooks to the galley' any minute," I said. "Let's get back down to the stores."

After hastily scraping our gear together, we set off – not a moment too soon. We met the Leading Seaman coming our way.

"Everything all right, lads?" he asked. "Did you get it finished?"

"Yes," we replied.

"Did you make a good job of it? The old boy is a bit fussy."

We thought we did, we told him.

"OK, lads, here are your cards. Put your gear back in the stores, and you can go."

"What the hell is that commander going to say when he sees it?" asked one of the party. "We shall all be on the bloody carpet, I reckon."

"Oh, I dunno," one of the others replied. "I've never seen that killick before, and I bet he hasn't seen me either – and he will never remember our names, will he?"

"We hope not," I said, "but suppose they tannoy us – what do we do then?"

Ignore it, we decided.

I never heard any more about it. Probably the next day another party was detailed off to clean the car up. I don't think the Leading Seaman would have recognised any of us again.

All the lads who were in Chatham Barracks will remember the eternal sweeping-up. I went on a number of scavenging and sweeping-up operations while I was there, and one in particular I thought was rather amusing.

We had swept and swept and swept again our area, and one lad threw his broom down and said, "I'm getting fed up with this. It's murder – bleeding ridiculous!"

A petty officer was in charge of our party on this occasion, but we had not sighted him since we started.

After a few more minutes, another lad said, "That's it – I've had enough. I'm going to find that petty officer and tell him we have finished."

He returned soon after, looking a bit crestfallen, and when we asked him if he had got our cards he replied, "No chance. That petty officer said, 'I haven't heard the pipe "hands to dinner", have you?' Of course I had to say no. 'Well then,' the bastard said, 'you haven't finished, have you? Carry on bleeding sweeping!'"

'Area sweeping' was soul-destroying, but I suppose they had to keep us occupied.

I went ashore at every opportunity – glad to get out for a few hours. I saw several shows in Chatham, and up in London, when we had all-night leave. Phyllis Dixey, the stripper, always packed the house.

I also had a long weekend at home. It was nice to see my family and old workmates again. I couldn't tell them very much as I had no idea where I might be going, although a strong buzz had been going the rounds about a large draft going to the Middle East shortly. My brother Arthur was already out there, I learned. My two younger sisters thought I looked smashing in my uniform!

The weekend passed all too quickly, and I caught the train back to London on the Sunday evening, spent the night at the Central Hall, Westminster, and caught an early train down to Chatham.

There were lots of gloomy faces around, and one chap in my compartment muttered, "Back to that bloody dump again! How do you feel when you walk in through that *Pembroke* gate?" he asked.

"My heart drops down into my boots," I replied, "and stays there until I come out again."

"Likewise," he muttered.

After checking in at the main gate, I thought I'd better go and have a look at the noticeboard, but there was no sign of my name. Back in my mess, I did not see one face I recognised. As I said earlier, men were coming and going all the time.

At the Monday morning muster I found that I'd been given 'area sweeping' again.

The following morning turned out to be a lot more interesting. I was one of a large party of men detailed off for a job in the dockyard. It turned out to be storing a ship – a big ship.

"What is she?" one of the chaps asked the leading seaman in charge of us when she came into view.

"Heavy cruiser," he replied. "HMS *London*. Town class," he added.

We thought her very impressive – the most powerful ship we had seen.

I got chatting to one of the crew members at 'stand easy', and he showed me around and told me a bit about her. The displacement was 10,000 tons, and she had a crew of about 700 men. The main armament was eight eight-inch guns.

Apparently, she had just completed a major refit, and our large party's job was to get a mass of stores aboard. This was the first warship I had set foot on. Five years later, she was also the last one I stepped off, and at this very same spot.

The weekend came round again, and still no draft. At Sunday morning divisions, the church parade was quite a spectacle. The navy band was marching and 'Heart of Oak' was echoing and re-echoing from the barrack blocks and the steep hillside behind them. I was to learn much about echoes later in the war.

Sometimes we would get sentry duty, or shore patrol. The latter was not a particularly enviable job, especially when we had to deal with men fighting drunk.

We had gas-mask drill frequently. I hated running around wearing a gas mask; I found it most difficult to breathe, but there was to be an occasion later on at sea when I wished I had been wearing one.

My name appeared on the noticeboard one morning with a whole host of others. Most of the day was spent going through the drafting routine – what a bind that used to be! – going round the various departmental offices, getting my chit of paper stamped, waiting for hours it seemed at 'K' Basement for medical checks, stripped down to our singlets and half frozen.

We packed our kitbags, lashed up our hammocks, and took

them down to the drill shed. They would be transported for us. We carried our personal belongings and toilet gear, etc. in a small suitcase. I don't think any of us were sorry to be leaving Chatham Barracks, but I'll wager a good many wished they were back there a few months later. There was much speculation as to our destination. The buzz which said we were to be sent to the Middle East proved to be correct.

CHAPTER 5

ON PASSAGE

Our journey began in the afternoon of the following day. Trucks took us to Chatham Station to catch a train to London. We felt like children let out to play – no constant looking over our shoulder, wondering if one of the barrack 'crushers' (barrack police) was about to pounce, on some pretext or other.

"Put your cap on straight!"

"Pull your collar down!"

"Button your coat!"

"Where is your gas mask?"

"Double up, that man!"

We hoped we had left all that behind us. We all understood the need for rules and regulations and discipline, naturally, but so much of it in the barracks was petty and needless, we thought.

Trucks transported us from Victoria to Euston Station, and we began the long journey to Scotland.

Arriving eventually at Glasgow, we were mustered in a large warehouse, where heads were counted. We were then marched to a dock, and boarded a troopship – one of the Union Castle liners. Not much conversion work had taken place at this still quite early stage of the war, and we thought she was quite magnificent.

We sailed the next morning. There was much activity in the yards down the Clyde, and a large convoy began to form up off the 'tail of the bank'. I was to spend some time around here, later in the war, and became very fond of this part of Scotland.

I felt very sad when the beautiful Holy Loch was defiled by the American nuclear obscenities that were 'planted' there.

There were several large liners in the convoy that was forming up, and I was able to discern the names of some of them: another Union Castle liner, the *Warwick Castle;* a French liner, *Louis Pasteur*; and the *Andes*, to name a few.

We had a bit of a scare that same evening when one of them collided with us. It didn't amount to very much, thankfully – just minor damage to the stern rails. It must have been a worrying time for the masters of those great ships, manoeuvring in those narrow waters. Several years later, the second ship I served on was involved in a collision, with much more serious consequences.

The long journey to the Middle East really began now as the convoy moved off down the firth past Bute, Arran, the lonely Ailsa Craig, and round the Mull of Kintyre to the open sea. This was a great experience for me, as I had never been to sea before.

Routine on board was quite free and easy. It was almost like a pleasure cruise really, as we had very little to do as regards duties. I think the chief and petty officers travelling with us were also pleased to relax and forget the rules and regulations.

Lifeboat stations were allocated, and we carried out boat drill every morning. We were directed to wear or carry our lifebelts at all times, and to be sure we could find our lifeboat stations in the dark.

The convoy went westwards for several days before turning to a more southerly course. I spent much of my time leaning over the rail, looking at the columns of ships, and the escorts beyond them. There were not very many of those, I thought. What a slaughter there would have been if the U-boats had found that convoy! There must have been several thousand men on those troopships.

I thought about home sometimes, and hoped my family were all right as there had been isolated bombing raids in the area. My old workmates were just beginning on the sugar-beet crop when I left. They were to get two land-girl helpers soon, to replace Arthur and me. A great job they did too for the remainder of the war, by all accounts.

It was quite a large farm – nearly 1,000 acres, employing twenty or so men and boys. There were about the same number of horses (mainly Suffolks) and one International tractor. Three horse keepers were employed, and they did the bulk of the ploughing, although sometimes one or two of the other chaps did a bit.

I had a go one day at ploughing, with three horses and a double-furrow plough – under the critical eye of the head horse keeper. Like most things, I found there was a bit more to it than meets the eye.

The horse keepers started work half an hour before the rest of us, to get their charges in and feed them – by the light of paraffin lamps in the wintertime. We started work early in those days – six thirty in the summer and seven o'clock in the winter – and worked a forty-eight-hour week, all for a few shillings.

The soil was light and easy to work, and plenty of manure was always available, from the horse, cattle and pig yards. A large flock of Suffolk ewes did the land good also.

All the fields on this farm were quite large; two of them in fact were over 100 acres. There was a particular reason for having large fields – or so one of the old horse keepers told me one day. He may have had his tongue in his cheek, I suspect, although I did not know what to make of it at the time – he told it so convincingly. It was all a question of decency, he said. It was all to do with testing the soil conditions in the springtime, with regard to sowing. The farmer would walk out into the middle of the field, drop his breeches and sit down – if it struck cold to his behind, he would decide to hang on for a week or two.

All a question of decency!

Very little artificial fertiliser was used on this farm, and spraying crops with weedkillers was unheard of.

People like to think back to the good old days, but they were not so good in some ways: long hours; hard physical work; and if you got soaking wet out in the fields, that was your hard luck

– you stayed like it till it was packing-up time.

The houses we lived in were terrible by today's standards, and not many landlords were anxious to improve them. Our old cottage had no facilities whatsoever, except for a small stove stuck up in one corner of the kitchen. There was a stone sink in another corner, with a waste pipe – but no tap. The tap was outside, between the two houses. The front, middle and back doors were in line with one another, and, standing on a hill as we were, completely exposed on all sides, the draught went completely through the house. Many times in the winter we sat with overcoats on, trying to keep warm.

How my mother managed with the washing for seven of us I will never know! It had to be done in a copper in an outhouse. First the copper had to be filled by bucket from the tap, which quite often in the winter had to be thawed out first. Then some sticks had to be chopped to heat the copper; and when Mother had finished her wash, it had to be bailed out.

Our kitchen had a stone floor, and Mother would buy the odd bit of coconut matting when she could afford it, so it didn't strike quite so cold in the winter. One day, when I was about seven or eight years old, Father brought two brand-new corn sacks home and spread them on the floor. We children were over the moon – we had some brand-new carpets!

They were hard times, but – all credit to my parents – we never went hungry. Father was a good gardener and kept us supplied with vegetables the whole year round. He also used to remedy the meat situation when the last of the joint had gone. He would go off with his old single-barrel twelve-bore and bring four or five pigeons home – other birds also sometimes – and, of course, there were always rabbits to be had. They were very healthy and plentiful in those days. I remember as I got a bit older going out at night with him, staking a long net out on the stubbles, and driving the rabbits into it. We would get several some nights. It used to be pitch-dark sometimes.

Father would say to me, "Stand at one end and rest your hand on top of the net – you will know when a rabbit hits it!" Sometimes we would change round, and I would walk the stubble, shaking a tin that held a small pebble – just enough noise to put the rabbits up.

Father had a few perks for his 'beer and baccy' money: surplus vegetables; rabbit, hare and mole skins; jays' feathers and pheasant tail feathers. These were some of the perks I know about. I wouldn't be at all surprised if there were others.

"It's a poor old job that hasn't got a few perks," I heard him say one time. Gardener and groom were his chief roles, but he was also handyman, mole catcher, vermin killer and, at odd times, stack thatcher.

Stack thatching was quite a big job. When all the corn had been carted and stacked there might be thirty or more stacks on a large farm. They would be threshed out in the wintertime. I quite enjoyed threshing time. It was something a bit different from the normal routine.

In the days before combine harvesters, all the corn was cut by self-binders, which tied the corn into sheaves and dropped them in rows. The men would then go round the field, grab one under each arm and set them up in shocks. After a while it would be carted by wagons and stacked. A horse-driven elevator was used to carry the sheaves up on to the stack, and a small mare had this task. She was hitched to a wooden arm underneath the elevator, and walked round and round in a small circle – a pretty monotonous job, I should think, but it was not very hard work for her really, and she had a little rest after each wagon was unloaded. It required a fair bit of skill to load a wagon, or build a stack.

"Keep the corners out, boy," the old hands would advise; "the middle will look after itself!"

Anyone who has had experience of either job will know how true the latter part of that remark is, especially when the sheaves were coming thick and fast.

Private contractors did the threshing on this farm. We used to be so excited as children when the tackle arrived – 'the farmer's band', we called it. Threshing drum, straw pitcher, chaff cutter and straw baler were all driven all drawn by a steam engine. Our particular contractor had Burnel engines, some single-cylinder, which made the distinctive 'chuff-chuff' sound; other contractors had compounds, which were quieter.

About a dozen men and boys would be employed at threshing time, some on the corn stacks. One of them would pass the sheaves up to a chap on the top of the drum, who cut the strings. The drum feeder, usually a contractor's man, would then feed the corn evenly into the drum. Sometimes a sheaf would go in uncut, and the drum would go 'whoomph' and the engine driver would cast up an anxious glance.

Two or three chaps would be employed in stacking the threshed-out straw, a boy would be bagging the chaff up, and one man at the front of the drum would be sacking the corn. This was carted to the barn, spread out and later dressed and weighed up, ready to be taken off to the miller.

The one remaining job was usually done by one of the boys. It entailed carting the wheat chaff to the stable chaff houses – wheat chaff was mixed with crushed oats for the horses' feed. The same boy also kept the engine supplied with coal and water. Oat and barley chaff was carted to the pit and burned, it being of no use.

The threshing drum did not smash up the straw as a combine harvester does, and much of it would be tied up to go to the racing stables in Newmarket. Large amounts were used for thatching purposes also.

Threshing was a dirty and dusty job sometimes, and often, especially in the case of wheat stacks, there would be a lot of rats to contend with. This reminds me of an amusing incident which happened one day. I don't think the chap it happened to thought it very funny, though.

We were threshing wheat at this time, and there were many rats – sometimes when a sheaf was lifted, two or three ran out. Anyway, one must have been passed in a sheaf up to old George on top of the drum. He let out a yell, and stood shaking one leg of his trousers. A rat had gone up one leg, round his crutch, and he was trying to shake it out down the other leg. He always wore his trousers at half-mast – we used to pull his leg about it, but it was a good thing he was that day, I think.

Poor old George lost his life in an accident on the farm towards the end of the war. An elevator used for loading the sugar beet fell on him. He died instantly.

Speaking of rats reminds me of a story my father told me many years ago. When he was a young lad, he and his father were out together late one winter night – he didn't say what errand they were on. They were walking along the lane when they heard a weird noise in the distance somewhere behind them, and the noise was getting louder by the minute. It was an awful sound, my father said, and he felt very frightened.

"Rats," his father said. "Run for the gate!"

They bolted to the end of the lane, where a five-barred gate led into a meadow. They climbed the gate and stood as high up as they could, and watched with horror as an army of rats passed beneath them, fighting and shrieking as they went. When they got down, my father was shaking like a leaf, and I think it scared my grandfather also. It must have been a very frightening experience indeed.

One more story about rats, and then I must get back to the war:

One old mongrel bitch we had, by the name of Judy, was a wonderful ratter. She never gave up. She would lie on the hearth, peeping out of one eye, watching for the slightest movement on my part towards the door.

"Are you ready?" I would say, or "Shall we go?" and she would leap up and wait at the door, whining to get out, tail wagging like mad.

We would go out with a powerful torch and a good heavy stick. I remember bitterly cold, frosty nights, trudging through deep snow, sometimes in bright moonlight and sometimes on nights as black as your hat. We would walk to where there were groups of stacks. We must have been mad, but we enjoyed it at the time, and Judy did too.

We would be out for perhaps two or three hours sometimes, maybe having killed up to about twenty rats. I would knock them down off the sides of the stacks, and Judy would snap them up, sometimes letting out a yelp when she got bitten by one of them. Often when we got back home, Judy would flop down on the floor completely exhausted, blood dripping from her nose or ears.

Father would scold her: "You silly old fool! Time you learned to get hold of them by their heads – not their arses!"

Judy would be ready and willing to go again the next night. That old bitch killed literally hundreds of rats in the twelve years or so we had her.

I had just one uncomfortable moment ratting. It was in one of the farm buildings one night. I was striking at a rat, as it ran up the stairs to the floor above, when it turned and leaped at my face. I threw my head to one side, and it hit my shoulder and fell to the floor. I decided to get out.

The convoy made steady progress to the south and it began to get much warmer. The voyage so far had been quite uneventful. We learned our first port of call would be Freetown in Sierra Leone. Notices appeared, warning the lads of the risks of sunbathing, but many lads chose to ignore them and got badly burned.

I was leaning over the stern rails watching the phosphorescence in the water, the night before we reached Freetown, when I thought I heard a dull thud. I wasn't absolutely certain – it could have been a noise on the ship itself, I thought – but a minute or so later the alarm bells went. On my way forward to my boat station, I noticed a faint glow out on the port side of the convoy, and when I arrived I noticed it had grown considerably brighter. It was obviously a ship on fire.

While we stood around awaiting any further orders, the sound of more dull thuds were heard.

"Destroyers depth-charging," remarked someone.

The torpedoed ship was blazing furiously by now, illuminating ships all around it – sitting ducks for the U-boat, I thought, if it was still around. Nothing further happened, and after about one hour we secured and fell out. All seemed very quiet again. The burning ship had fallen well astern of the convoy by now.

"Destroyers will probably sink it," said someone.

It was our first glimpse of the war at sea.

Early the following morning, we had what was for many of us our first glimpse of a foreign land. A whole crowd of lads were hanging over the port-side rails, eagerly peering into the mist. It was already quite warm and the water was mirror-smooth.

Presently someone shouted, "Look over there!"

Our eyes followed the pointing finger, and there above the bank of mist was the faint outline of a hillside, and a little while later we could pick out the shapes of clumps of trees, and then individual trees. It was a very exciting moment.

An hour or so later we were at anchor. The mist cleared quickly as the sun began to climb higher, and it was becoming quite hot. We noticed an armada of small boats approaching, and as they got nearer we could see just one occupant in each.

"Reception committee?" asked someone. "I wonder what they want."

We soon found out: money. We threw coins and they dived for them – and how those chaps could dive and swim! They would sit there gazing up at us, paddling with their hands to hold the boats against the current, watch a coin as it fell into the water, then half fall out of the canoe and dive after it. It might be several seconds before they surfaced, holding the coin between their lips.

How they managed to scramble back in their boats again without capsizing them I will never know. Then they would sit there waiting and watching, paddling with their hands, and baling out with one foot.

"Glasgow tanner, Jack" (silver sixpence) they would shout up to us.

A good many sixpences were dropped. I don't know how many of them they retrieved – possibly Freetown Harbour bottom is littered with lost coins.

When the coin collectors decided they had got about as much as they were likely to get they regrouped, so to speak, and departed for the shore. The fruit sellers came out then – larger boats this time, with two or three occupants and a load of luscious fruits. They did a roaring trade. After more than two weeks at sea, fresh fruit of any kind was more than welcome. Baskets on the ends of heaving lines were going up and down along the ship's side like yo-yos.

I was to come back to this place several times later in the war, and had a few trips ashore. We would buy whole stalks of green bananas in the hope of taking a few of them home to our families. Bananas were one of the many things unobtainable back home.

Various compartments of the ship were tried out for storage, but usually most of them ripened and had to be eaten long before we got back to the UK. A lot depended on whether it would be a fast or slow convoy. However, on two occasions I did get a few home to my family. Needless to say, they were very pleased. This was when I was on my second ship. Meanwhile I was on my way to join my first. Our next ports of call were Cape Town and Durban – two fine cities and a lovely climate, we thought. We were sickened and disgusted by the race segregation – everywhere we looked were signs and notices: 'Europeans Only' or 'No Coloured'.

I was fascinated by the rickshaw boys. They were most picturesque, with their huge ostrich-plume headdresses. They reminded me of race days in Newmarket, and Prince Monolulu, the racing tipster. I saw him many times with the three feathers in his headband.

"I've got a horse" was his cry.

I remember Prince Monolulu for one other thing also: a wreath he sent to the funeral of a racing personality of the period bore the inscription 'On and under the turf all men are equal.' How very true!

We changed ships at Durban, and it was quite a business getting all the kitbags and hammocks up from below, and sorting through them to find one's own and make sure it was not left behind. We then had to hump them along the quay to another berth and load them again.

We now had another ship to find our way around. My living

quarters were on one deck, and boat stations were on a different deck on the opposite side. However, I managed.

We stayed in Durban one more day while the hull was spray-painted. This ship was a luxury French liner, and she took us for the remainder of our journey up to the Red Sea and Suez.

Up till now it had seemed like a great adventure, but soon we were going to be in the war. It was a sobering thought.

CHAPTER 6

MALTA CONVOYS

A shrill on the bosun's pipe came over the Tannoy: "Do you hear, there? This is the Captain speaking. The ship will be putting to sea at 1800 hours. Later we shall rendezvous with a small fleet of supply ships and proceed to the westward. That is all."

An immediate murmur broke out on the mess deck, and anxious faces looked at one another.

"Proceeding to the westward!" exclaimed a voice. "What kind of crap is that? Why don't he come out with it straight, and say we are going to Malta!"

"Pipe down, stupid!" replied someone. "We don't need reminding."

Men showed their anxiety in different ways. Some would sit silently, deep in their thoughts; others would laugh and crack the most ridiculous jokes.

"If those Stukas decide to drop a bomb on your head, Alf, can I have that pile of dirty books in your locker?" another voice piped up.

"What's the address of that party you were telling me about, Smiler? It's on the cards she might be needing a different pair of hands on her tits after this trip!"

Some would sit and write letters home: "If I don't make it, chum, see that my missus gets this," and letters would be exchanged.

Men whose action stations were in exposed positions, or in the gun turrets, checked that their gear was to hand – steel helmets, earplugs and anti-flash gear. All would check their lifebelts.

The Tannoy crackled again, and then the bosun's pipe: "Close all X and Y doors. Close all scuttles and deadlights. Special sea dutymen close up. Hands will go to dusk action stations at 2100 hours."

The ship trembled slightly as the screws began to turn, and we slipped from the buoy and headed for the harbour entrance, and the open sea beyond.

Some time later: "Secure action stations. Defence watch, close up."

My own defence (cruising) and action station, at this particular time, was in the tower steering position, three decks down, in the heart of the ship. In wartime, the bridge wheelhouse was not used.

Three of us would be down there – a quartermaster and two telegraph men – and we would take the wheel in turn for the four-hour watch. We steered by a gyrocompass repeater, but there was also a Sperry and a magnetic compass.

I was quite excited when I took the wheel for the first time – me, a country boy who had never steered anything more than a team of three horses or a bicycle, on the wheel of one of His Majesty's light cruisers! It gave me quite a thrill when I could feel the ship alive in my hands. It required the fullest concentration, and the crucial thing was not to allow the ship to stray off course. A vehicle on a flat surface will continue in a straight line, but a ship certainly will not.

When the sea was on the quarter, or right astern, it could be a very testing job indeed. You had to anticipate the ship veering off to one side, quickly put on several degrees of opposite wheel, and maybe as quickly take it off again.

I well remember one occasion in particular when we had a choppy following sea. The other telegraph man said to me when I took over, "You will have to watch the cow – she's all over the bleeding place."

I soon found out he hadn't exaggerated. In less time than it takes to tell, we were off course by about twenty degrees to port. I brought her carefully back.

'Must not overcorrect,' I was telling myself, 'or you will be off across to the other side!'

'Chasing the ship's head' they called it – a fatal mistake. It could cause the ship to develop a nasty rolling motion, to the discomfort of everyone. There would be some choice remarks on the mess decks.

"What kind of bloody lunatic is on the wheel!"

Anyway, we were back on course; but within seconds, it seemed, we were about twenty degrees off to port again.

"See what I mean!" grinned my fellow telegraph man, who was watching over my shoulder.

I brought her back again, and found she would hover more or less on course for a little while, and would then want to slide off to port again as the motion of the sea pushed her stern to starboard. After a little while, I found I could anticipate this, quickly put on about twenty degrees of starboard wheel, hold it for a few seconds, and then back to midships. She stayed practically dead on course, and I felt on top of the world – more so when a voice came down the voice pipe from the compass platform.

"This is the Captain speaking. Who is on the wheel?"

I gave my name, and he said, "Very good steering."

The steering gear was operated by a hydraulic system – using a mixture of glycerine and water. Massive pistons in the tiller flat moved the rudder over. One could plainly hear the hum down in the after part of the ship. There was also an emergency crossing position down aft.

We had to be on our toes when under air attack. Any second there was liable to be an emergency order for wheel and telegraphs, such as "Full astern port", "Full astern starboard" or "Hard port".

We really had to move fast then. The ship would keel over as she slewed round, and a bomb or stick of bombs would fall where a few seconds earlier the ship had been. Unfortunately, for some ships it didn't work out that way.

It was very disconcerting serving below decks, as I remember from my time in the magazine crew. We could only guess what was happening up top.

On one occasion we carried out a bombardment of some of Rommel's armour at Halfaya Pass. Helmsmanship needed to be very precise for this kind of operation, and for that reason the chief quartermaster took over.

I had the first watch this night (8 p.m. till midnight), which meant I would not get very much sleep as it would be dawn action stations at about 5 a.m. This might last for a short time only, if we were lucky, or it could be for several hours, or even all day.

My next watch on would be the forenoon (8 a.m. till noon), as we were on the three-watch system. After the forenoon, I would be on again for the last dog watch (6 p.m. till 8 p.m.). The early evening watch (4 p.m. till 8 p.m.) was split into two parts – the first and last dog watches. This was in order to vary the times each watch was on duty.

My next shift after the last dog watch would be the morning watch (4 a.m. till 8 a.m.), then the first dog watch (4 p.m. till 6 p.m.). After that would come the middle watch (midnight till 4 a.m.), and, to complete the cycle, the afternoon watch (noon till 4 p.m.).

On most of the smaller ships, it was watch and watch – four hours on, and four hours off. I often thought how tiring that must have been, especially during very long periods at sea. I didn't have to find out, as it happened, as each of my three ships was on the three-watch system.

Midnight came, and the end of the watch. I went up on deck for a breath of fresh air before I turned in. It was bright moonlight, and I could plainly see the four ships we were to escort to the westward.

A few days later, I had two new jobs. I was put in starboard pom-pom crew (a new action station this), and I was also taken off normal part-of-ship duties and made a petty-officers'-mess man.

The latter was a nice quiet little number. There were three of us, and I was pleased to see my old friend Stripey was to be in charge. Our duties were to keep the mess generally clean and tidy, and to fetch the meals from the galley, and dish them up.

It was here I met for the first time the chief gunner's mate who was the captain of 'A' turret.

I said to him one day, as I handed him his dinner, "I was down in your magazine for a spell."

We had a chat and he asked what my present action station was.

When I said up on pom-pom, he exclaimed, "Sod that – too bloody exposed up there! If you like, I will get you transferred to my turret."

I thanked him, but said, "I don't think I would fancy that either." Maybe I was remembering what happened to the *Orion*'s 'A' turret.

We had a nasty moment in the mess pantry one dinner time, I recall. One of us had brought a huge dish of steaming-hot minced beef from the galley, and for some reason or other it came off the worktop and landed upside down on the deck!

Quick as a flash Stripey slammed down the serving hatch and we quickly scooped it back into the dish. We didn't have any complaints about that day's dinner, and the pantry floor was pretty clean.

Being petty-officers'-mess men, we were excused cruising/ defence stations; it was a welcome relief from those four-hour stints.

At about this time we had a bit of a respite. We and one of our sister ships were ordered to Haifa, in what was then Palestine, a British protectorate. I think it was something to do with forestalling German intentions in Syria and the consequent threat to our oil supplies and oil terminals at Haifa itself. Anyway, it was a welcome break, and whilst we were there a bus trip was organised to Nazareth. We saw the carpenter's shop and the cave Jesus is said to have occupied. I'm afraid most of us rather disgraced ourselves whilst we were there. Either the wine was bad, or it was more potent than we thought.

When it was time to start the journey back, we discovered that two of our party were missing, and when we finally found them – completely flaked out – it meant that we were going to be late getting back to the ship.

The journey was pretty hair-raising, to say the least. We were extremely lucky to get back at all, I think. The narrow road winding over the hills was atrocious in parts. At times there would be a steep hill on one side, and a steeper precipice on the other, and numerous hairpin bends, each one inviting disaster.

A few of the lads, more sober than most of us, realising we were going to be adrift if we didn't hurry, were urging the Arab driver on: "Faster – faster, John!"

He sat crouched over the steering wheel, a wide grin on his face, horn blaring every few seconds.

Some of the lads were lying pretty well senseless across the seats, and on the floor; others were hanging out of the sides – sick as dogs. It was disgusting. Another group, in the back of the bus, burst into song after a while – various naval ballads, and one of the more filthy versions of 'Maggie May'.

We arrived back at Haifa two hours or so late, and found a patrol waiting for us. The petty officer in charge got us fallen in after a fashion. His gimlet eyes moved from man to man, his expression of disgust increasing all the time.

"God Almighty!" he breathed; then his gaze settled on Ginger and me.

I should have mentioned that we two had availed ourselves of Arab headdresses in Nazareth, and had travelled back wearing them. Thankfully we had recovered ourselves enough to remove them before getting off the bus – then we realised we didn't have our caps. Anyway, there stood Ginger and I, bareheaded and feeling mighty small, under the scornful glare of the Petty Officer.

How smart the patrol looked, I thought, and we were a scruffy ragbag!

"Put your caps on," the Petty Officer ordered.

"We haven't got them, Petty Officer," I said.

"No," echoed Ginger, "we haven't."

"Where are your caps?"

The question came in a cold and ominous tone, the words slow and measured.

"I think we left them in Nazareth," stuttered Ginger.

I thought the Petty Officer was going to explode when he heard that.

"Oh no!" he grated. "I don't bloody believe it!"

I wouldn't have been a bit surprised if he had drawn his revolver and shot us there and then.

There were a few chuckles from the other lads, but they soon ceased when he glared at them.

He turned back to Ginger and me. His voice was calm – deceptively calm – when he spoke.

"Correct me if I'm wrong," he said, "but I thought just for a moment you said your caps were in Nazareth. I surely must have misunderstood!" His eyes bored into mine. "Well?" he snapped.

"That is where they are, Petty Officer." I just about managed to get the words out.

"I see," he replied, quite mildly. "Now would you mind explaining why your caps are in Nazareth, and not here in Haifa and on your heads?"

'I'm not going to reply to that,' I thought. 'I'm not going to say, "Because we gave them away to a couple of Arabs." I hope Ginger comes up with something.'

"They must have fallen off, and we didn't notice," said Ginger with a look of desperation on his face.

The Petty Officer gave him a withering look and snapped, "I see – and you seem to think I have just fallen off a bloody log! You two are in the shit – in the shit right up to your eyeballs, up the creek without a bloody paddle – don't make it any worse than it is already!"

There was some more chuckling from the other lads.

He rounded on them savagely: "You are all in the shit," he bellowed. "Look at the state of you! It looks like you have been rolling around in the gutter, spewing all over each other. Disgrace to the service – that's what you are – the whole bleeding lot of you."

"We had too much to drink, Petty Officer," I said, "and must have fallen over and lost our caps."

He calmed down somewhat and addressed us all: "You are over two hours adrift – do you realise what that would have meant if the ship had sailed? Just suppose the ship had been ordered out," he continued, "and was attacked by a dirty great heap of dive-bombers. What is the Chief Gunner's Mate going to say when the Captain says, 'I say – those guns, old boy – only half the bally armament seems to be firing.' What has he got to tell him? It's because the crews of the other half are rolling around Nazareth, as pissed as newts! Right then – back to the ship, and God help the lot of you."

The outcome of all this was two weeks' stoppage of leave and pay, and an extra week for Ginger and me.

We two each faced four charges: (1) being two hours and twelve minutes adrift; (2) being improperly dressed; (3) misappropriating government property; and (4) letting the service down.

We deserved all we got, I think.

"Have you heard the latest buzz, Matt," asked one of my messmates the following morning. "Came from one of the Signals lot, so our leading hand said, so you can bet it's right."

"So what is the buzz, then?" I asked.

"We ain't going back on the Malta run," was the reply. "We're going down through the canal."

"Where to then?" I asked.

"Dunno, Matt – he didn't say any more than that."

Sure enough, down through the Suez Canal we went, a day or so later. All kinds of rumours – buzzes, we called them – were going round the mess decks. Favourites among them were 'out East somewhere' and 'down to Durban for a refit'.

The official explanation when we got it was quite different: we were to escort troopships up the Red Sea, to Suez. Apparently, masses of stores, tanks and equipment of all kinds had been pouring into Egypt, to re-equip the desert armies after the disaster of Greece and Crete. Also, during the next few weeks, thousands of fresh troops would be arriving. We were to see, for the first time, the great liners *Queen Elizabeth* and *Queen Mary* among others.

It seemed the operations had not escaped the notice of the German Air Force, and many attacks had been made on the mass of shipping, and the ports of Suez, Ismailia and Port Said. Parachute mines had been dropped on a number of occasions, and the canal itself had been partly blocked.

My first sightings of the *Queen Elizabeth* and *Queen Mary* were breathtaking. We passed quite close to both of them. They were massive. The former could carry 15,000 and the latter 10,000 men at a time, we learned. Both ships made many crossings of the Atlantic, and other oceans throughout the war – completely unescorted. They relied on their speed for protection against the U-boats.

One day we crossed the wake of the *Queen Elizabeth* about two miles astern of her, and we were tossed about like a cork in a bathtub – she had churned the water up so much.

While we were in the Red Sea, one of those more objectionable notices appeared on the boards. I don't know whether it was designed to stir up ill feeling, but it certainly had that effect. It began:

> The ship's company is hereby informed.
> The supply of fresh water will be strictly limited,
> and will be turned off for specified periods.

'Fair enough,' we thought. 'With the terrible heat, there will be an increased demand, and the ship can only supply us with a certain amount.'

The next part of the notice caused a laugh:

> Sea water is to be used for toilet and washing of gear.
> Salt water soap will be issued for that purpose.

"Who do they reckon they're kidding?" said someone. "We all know bloody well it doesn't work!"

The last part of the notice incensed us:

71

Orders have been given for holes to be drilled in the officers' baths, five inches from the bottom.

There was an angry outburst when we read it. "Bloody diabolical!" was the general comment. That they should be permitted to bath at all with fresh water, let alone have five inches of it!

"How many blokes' allowance is that?" asked one lad. "Ten? Twenty?"

"For each one to bathe his lily-white body in!" muttered another. "I hate those bloody pigs more now than I did before, and that's saying something!"

Even in adversity, the 'them and us' thing seemed to prevail.

The heat in the Red Sea was overpowering at times. The upper works of the ship would get to hot to touch. I remember sitting down below on the mess deck, clad only in shorts with a towel round my waist to catch the perspiration as it rolled down. Although there was often a strong breeze blowing, it was hot and full of dust. An awful place!

We had several runs ashore in Suez, and returning to the ship from one of them one night became quite alarming, but at the same time quite comical.

The night was pitch-dark, and a strong breeze was blowing, making the water quite choppy. Our motor cutter was waiting for us at the jetty. How the coxswain had found his way there in these conditions mystified me, but, more to the point, how was he going to find his way back again?

Our ship lay at anchor out in the bay, somewhere.

There was near disaster when we cast off. Everyone who has messed about in boats knows that the first priority is to see the load is distributed evenly. You trim the boat.

The blokes piled aboard. A large party, the worse for drink, collapsed in a heap and lay there. A good two-thirds of the cargo of men were on the side of the boat nearest the jetty. The coxswain was doing his best to get some to move over – without much success.

"We're not moving till some of you stupid bastards get across to the other side," he shouted.

Some were beginning to lose their patience.

"Come on, 'Swain – let's get moving. We'll be here all bloody night! Let go those ropes, somebody."

We cast off, and several hands began to push the cutter away from the jetty, which had been supporting that side of her. We keeled over immediately, to an alarming angle. One side was about four feet above the water, and the other about four inches!

The coxswain, a leading seaman, went almost berserk: "Trim the boat, you bloody lunatics!"

Several blokes did scramble over, but there was still a large group on the port side.

"Sodden with booze!" muttered a burly stoker sitting alongside me. "I'll sober the bastards up."

He moved gingerly across the thwart to the nearest one, who lay with his head and shoulders partly over the gunwale. Placing his hand on the back of the man's head, he pushed his face down in the water, held it there for a second or two, let him up, and then pushed him down again. He came up coughing and spluttering.

"Now do what the coxswain tells you," said the Stoker. "Get across to the other bleeding side!"

The Stoker grabbed the shoulder of another one. "You too!" he shouted. "Move your bloody self!"

One or two more, and the cutter was on a fairly even keel.

"You blokes up in the bow," shouted the coxswain, "keep your eyes peeled for a ship – any ship," he added.

I had no idea where we were, which direction we were going in, or where our ship lay, but presently one of the lookouts shouted a warning: "Ship ahead!"

The coxswain cut the engine and allowed the boat to drift alongside.

A voice hailed us: "Boat ahoy! Who are you, and what do you want?"

"We are looking for the flagship," replied the coxswain.

"Well, you're wasting your time looking here, mate," came the reply. "This ain't it."

"Can you give us an idea which direction she's in?" the coxswain asked.

The beam of the torch was shone down at us, and then waved up ahead.

"She's up there, mate – somewhere," called the voice. "Best of luck to you!"

We got under way again, and a few minutes later another shape loomed out of the darkness. The engine was stopped again.

"A bleeding merchant packet!" exclaimed someone. "No use asking them – might be foreigners anyhow."

We started off again, and presently one of the chaps in the bow shouted a warning. It was a rope slung between two small buoys, and we moved slowly along underneath it – passing it overhead from hand to hand. A little further on, we repeated the manoeuvre – another rope had been slung between buoys.

"What the hell was that?" asked a voice. "Where are we?"

"Bloody hell!" exclaimed someone. "You know what it was: Jerry has been dropping parachute mines, and our lot have been marking their positions with these buoys. I reckon we just went over one of the leaders!"

We found our ship soon afterwards, and although we were about half an hour adrift it was overlooked. The coxswain's explanation was accepted.

A day or two later we returned to Alexandria, and in the evening of the day of arrival we slipped from our buoy to escort another convoy to the westward.

"It ain't natural," remarked Steve. "Hermann has never been this late before."

"You don't need to sound so bleeding miserable," replied Ginger. "Cheer up, me old mate. Hermann will be along soon enough!"

"Yeah, that's right," said Taff Morgan. "He hasn't let us down yet, has he?"

"Bleeding lot of idiots!" muttered Leading Seaman Ashby, the gun captain.

It was dawn action stations on the starboard pom-poms, and we were all wondering what was happening – or, more to the point, what was not happening.

Usually, the German shadower was sizing us up long before now. A tiny speck would be sighted, moving low over the horizon, gradually growing in size till it was recognisable as an aircraft, and he would fly up and back on our beam – keeping well out of range of our guns. Then maybe he would circle right around us, and fly up and down on the other side, no doubt checking our position and course, and sending the information back to his 'nasty little friends', as Steve would put it.

"Perhaps he had a run ashore last night and got pissed up," said Ginger. "He's having a lie-in this morning," he added.

"Or maybe he went with one of those Sicilian tarts and got poxed up," offered Steve.

"I hope he got pissed up and poxed up," said Taff.

"Cut the cackle, you lot," said Petty Officer Simpson, "and keep your eyes peeled."

"We are keeping our eyes peeled," said Steve. "We can still bleeding well talk, can't we – or ain't that allowed?"

"Don't get stroppy," said the Petty Officer.

"Get stuffed!" muttered Ginger. "Bleeding petty officers – too many of them by half."

"Hermann is late," said Taff. "I wonder what is going on – maybe it's like Steve said: Hermann has caught the boat up. Could be he's seeing his quack this very minute," he added with a laugh.

There followed a comic conversation between Steve and Ginger:

"What is your trouble this morning, young Hermann?"

"Well, Doctor, I went ashore last night and got pissed up."

"I suppose the whole sodding lot of you did the same," said the quack. "Don't waste me bleeding time!"

"But, Doc," said young Hermann, "I met up with one of those Sicilian tarts and did something what I didn't oughter."

"Ho ho, young Hermann! You were a naughty, dirty little boy, weren't you? Too bad! Right now, your Uncle Hermann in Berlin wants you to go and check on that Brit convoy."

"But, Doc, ain't you going to do anything?"

"Nothing I can do at this stage, young Hermann. Take a couple of aspirins – if it starts to shrivel up, come and see me again!"

The little sketch caused great amusement. Anything was welcome to break the tension.

"Stupid lot of bleeders!" muttered Leading Seaman Ashby.

"I reckon we're all getting bomb happy," said Taff.

Both Steve and his close friend Ginger were jokers. Perhaps it was their way of keeping their sanity. The nerves of many men on the Malta convoys were shot to pieces, and some men, in fact, had to be replaced.

I recall when I was a petty-officers'-mess man, how some of them would dash to their lockers when the bugle blared out 'action stations'. Out would come the little bottles of rum, and they would gulp some down before they dashed out.

"Getting their little bit of Dutch courage!" Stripey would say with a grin.

It is very difficult to describe the feeling when action stations was sounded, when we heard the urgent bugle call over the Tannoy, followed by the bosun's pipe, and the order, "Hands to action stations." Every sense became alert – every nerve tingling, and a curious feeling in the stomach.

"What stupid blighter called them butterflies?" said one of the lads one day, when we were talking about it. "They are more like elephants in mine."

"I reckon it's how criminals feel when they go to the gallows," Taff said.

I think he might have had a point, because it was in the mind of every man that within minutes or even seconds of the bugle call some or all of us could be dead or mutilated – and that call was sounded off on every Malta convoy, many times.

Once the action started you forgot it all. There was a curious feeling of elation, as though you were walking on air. Exhausted as we may have become, we kept going; and the harder the going got, the more determined we became. When the action was over, we might find our hands trembling uncontrollably. I don't suppose anyone who has never been under a concentrated air attack could begin to understand. Everyone who has certainly will.

Steve was off again now: "Salvation Army!" he bawled. "January, February, March! Sister Anna will carry the banner."

"I carried it last week," protested Ginger in a squeaky little female voice.

"You will carry it again this week," said Steve.

"But I'm in the family way," squeaked Ginger.

"You are in everybody's way," roared Steve. "Get out of it!"

On the deck a packing ring; on top of that, the GI's hat.

"Alarm bearing red forty degrees!"

Everyone's manner changed immediately; all of us were instantly alert and ready.

"It's over on the other side," joked Ginger. "None of our business."

"That's enough – on the gun," Leading Seaman Ashby snapped.

We watched as the three forward turrets trained round to a point just forward of the port beam, their gun barrels cocked high in the air. The port-side pom-poms were also moving on to the bearing.

Gunfire came from the port-side destroyer screen. We could see the flashes and puffs of smoke from their 4.5s, and almost immediately our 5.25s opened up. A flash and a cloud of smoke leaped from the barrels. Seconds later we saw the shell bursts – little puffs of cotton wool. Some appeared white, others brownish.

We on the pom-pom mounting donned steel helmets, anti-flash gear, and earplugs. We had not sighted any aircraft yet, but any second now we could be in action.

"Christ Almighty!" shouted Taff. "Look!"

We all spotted them in the same instant, I think.

"One-elevens – high-level lot," said Petty Officer Simpson. "Keep your eyes peeled for dive-bombers, lads!"

Our shooting looked pretty good – dead in line, and slightly ahead of the formation, but of course we couldn't tell how it was for height. Our three sister cruisers had now joined in, and there was a terrific barrage going up. Shells were bursting all around the aircraft. I quite expected to see several of them come tumbling down, but, as Leading Seaman Ashby had said, "There is a hell of a lot of sky up there!"

Our own mounting was silent, as the aircraft were well beyond the effective range of our guns.

A forest of bomb splashes rose around and beyond the single ship we were escorting, but she seemed to come through them unscathed. An old friend, this ship, we had escorted her several times – a fast merchantman, converted to carry fuel oil and aviation spirit for Malta's Spitfires.

We had been told that the situation at Malta was becoming desperate, and that it was absolutely vital we got this ship through.

I looked up at the sky again as cheering broke out, and I saw two of the attackers come spiralling down, smoke pouring from one of them.

"That's the end of the war for them," said Leading Seaman Ashby.

"Probably the end of everything else as well," said the Petty Officer.

The remaining aircraft made a wide turn out on the starboard side, and came in for a second run, still way above the range of our pom-poms.

"Bloody bystanders – that's what we are," moaned Ginger.

As gun layer on the mounting, I imagine he was itching to get his sights on them.

"I'm not complaining," said Taff, who was one of the loaders. "I'm just hoping there aren't any dive-bombers up there."

It was quite obvious it was the supply ship they were after. She was completely obscured from view within seconds by the great spouts of water that rose up all around her.

She emerged again, safely it seemed, and ploughed majestically on. We all heaved a great sigh of relief. It didn't seem possible she'd come through that unscathed.

The action only lasted a few minutes, and then an uneasy calm settled over us.

'What is coming next?' we wondered. 'We are not likely to get off as easy as that.'

We stayed closed up for the remainder of the morning, but no further attacks developed, although we were being shadowed the whole time. The screening destroyers loosed off a few rounds at them, now and again, when they ventured too close.

We were divided into two groups. "Half of you keep your eyes peeled," said Petty Officer Simpson; "the rest of you relax, but don't leave the gun deck. Change round each half-hour."

I sat in the shade during my rest periods, half dozing at times, but my thoughts wandered between home and what was happening around me. It was quite unbelievable really how quickly one could change and adapt from one life to the other. Already, after a few months only, I felt quite a seasoned warrior.

At home, before the war, life had been quite orderly, and, in the main, uneventful. It was a different story on the Malta convoys. You never knew from one minute to the next what was going to happen, and you wondered many times if the next minute was going to be your last. I had been thrown into the deep end at HMS *Ganges*, and also into the war at sea, it seemed.

We 'hostilities only' sailors had been looked upon as impostors at first by the regular navy men (quite understandable, I suppose), but gradually we had become accepted. By the end of the war, of course, we had become the great majority.

Our journey out from the UK had been quite uneventful really. We had disembarked at Suez, and had travelled through Egypt by train to Alexandria. The journey had taken all night, and was something best forgotten. The carriages had wooden benches and no glass in the window openings, and we in our tropical rig were frozen stiff. I wouldn't have believed the nights could be so cold where by day the heat was at times unbearable. Every few miles the train stopped, or slowed to walking pace, and a horde of fruit and lemonade sellers jumped on board – and off again at the next stop.

It seemed at times the journey would never end, but we finally arrived at Alexandria, cold, hungry and pretty miserable. We were shepherded into trucks, which took us to a tented camp a few miles out. Here we would stay, while awaiting ~~draughts~~ to various ships. *drafts*

We were advised to rake the sand over each night before spreading our hammocks out to turn in.

"You don't want any snakes or scorpions as bedfellows," said the chief petty officer in charge of us.

We were not very impressed with our introduction to Egypt. A land of flies, sand and smells, I will always remember it as. That fine sand seemed to get everywhere. I was still finding it in my gear and kitbag for some time after I had left the Mediterranean station about a year later.

Our meals were eaten out in the open, and it was a near-impossible job keeping the flies off our food. In the town, we saw babies and old men lying asleep in doorways and alleyways, their mouths and eyes black with clusters of flies. It made us feel sick.

We used to buy chameleons ashore later on, and take them back to the ship, where we would put them on the mess table and watch them catching flies. They seemed such slow and ungainly creatures, but their tongues would snake out like lightning and snatch flies off the table.

The smells didn't bear thinking about in town – open sewers in the poorer parts of the city, and native cooking.

"I don't know which smells worse," my old friend Stripey had said.

There were swarms of young boys in Alexandria. Some of them wanted to clean our boots, others to sell us dirty books and pictures, and the remainder clearly wanted us to go home and meet their sisters.

"Very nice, Jack – very young – very tasty!"

In the navy in wartime, and the other services as well, I expect, you are liable to meet all kinds of characters. In our camp there was a concrete-and-brick administration building, also housing the guardroom, armoury, and a couple of cells. Here one evening I was detailed off for cell sentry duty for the first watch (8 p.m. till midnight). There was just one occupant

– I had no idea what he was in detention for.

"No contact; no talking with the prisoner," the other sentry informed me when I relieved him, but he had hardly gone out through the door when the prisoner spoke to me.

"You got a fag, sentry?" he asked.

'I'm not supposed to talk – better ignore him,' I thought.

"What's the matter with you, then – got bloody cloth ears or something? I asked if you've got a fag!"

"I don't smoke," I said.

"Likely story that," he replied. "Come on – they ain't going to know."

"I don't smoke," I repeated.

He was silent for a minute or two, then asked if I had been out there long.

"No," I replied.

"What ship you off, then?"

"I'm waiting for my first ship," I said.

"Bloody good luck to you, chum – you'll need it. It's murder out there."

There was silence again for several minutes. Then he asked what I did before I got called up.

"I volunteered," I replied.

"Dead keen, eh? King and country – all that crap."

"Something like that," I said. "I worked on a farm," I added. "What did you do?"

"Spell in Wormwood Scrubs," he replied. "Smash and grab!" He grinned and added, "That was me occupation, so to speak."

I was curious to know why he was in detention, and finally asked him.

"Hit a copper with a bottle," he replied. "They say I killed him – don't know whether I did or not, but he was still lying there when the patrol lugged me out. The bastards don't fight fair," he muttered.

"What do you mean?" I asked. "Who don't?"

"Bastard coppers," he replied.

"I don't know what you are talking about," I said.

"I'll tell you what happened, then. I was in this bar, see. Posh

81

sort of place it was – not like the bloody dives us matelots generally go to. Waiters all ponced up in monkey suits, napkins hanging over their bleeding arms – you know what I mean. Well, I was sat at a table, and this tart comes over. Well, she wasn't a tart – not like what we mean. I suppose she was one of those bleeding hostesses. You know what I mean," he went on: "they keep smiling at you while they're getting you to empty your bleeding wallet. But I wanted more than smiles, if you know what I mean. Anyhow, she kept fobbing me off.

"'Later,' she kept saying. 'Another bottle of wine, shall we?'

"Well, I was getting fed up with this – it was costing me a packet.

"'I'll find out what your bleeding game is,' I thought.

"I clapped one arm around her shoulder and pulled her close, and stuck my other hand up her leg. She went bloody berserk. Over went the table as she tore herself loose.

"'Pig! English pig!' she kept shouting.

"'You are a bloody bitch,' I bellowed back at her.

"Then I spotted this big geezer making for me. I'd noticed him standing there watching.

"'Bouncer,' I thought.

"I snatched a bottle off the next table as he got close.

"'I'll give you bloody bouncer,' I said, and smashed it down across his head.

"Well, he went down as though he had been poleaxed!

"Somebody must have called the cops. There was two of the bleeders coming at me. I downed the first one, but the other got me." He fingered the dressing high up on the side of his head, and muttered, "Bleeding coppers! They don't fight fair – the bastards use sticks!"

"What do you think will happen to you?" I asked.

"Dunno – ninety days chokey for sure. Maybe they will hang me," he said with a laugh. "Dunno, mate, and don't care much."

He was a hard case!

Alexandria was a fascinating city I thought, a place of great contrasts. A few of the people looked very wealthy and elegant, but I'll bet the great majority didn't possess much more than the rags they stood up in.

I well remember my first run ashore.

Stripey had warned us of some of the dangers: "Don't go straying down the back alleys alone. Don't get yourselves picked up by the whores," he said. "Go to the recognised places. Never pay the price they ask in the shops – you barter for everything!"

We found the latter to be very good advice.

Stripey had agreed to come with a small party of us: "I'd better come along and show you the ropes" – he grinned – "and keep an eye on you!"

I think he regarded us as his 'wingers' and himself as a father figure.

In one of the shops, one of the lads took a fancy to a particular little ornament.

"I'd like to take that home for my old lady," he remarked. "She collects this sort of thing."

"Leave it to me," Stripey said.

He turned to the proprietor, who stood there smiling in anticipation.

"How much are you asking for the little vase?" asked Stripey.

"A hundred piastres, Jack," he replied, with a disarming grin on his face.

"Not bleeding likely!" snapped Stripey. "I'll give you 50, you thieving bastard."

"No, no, Jack – worth more," was the response.

"Well, you ain't getting it," said Stripey.

"For you, Jack, 90 piastres" – still with that little grin on his face.

"Get knotted," said Stripey. "I'll give you 60, and not a bleeding penny more."

"No, no, Jack – worth more. For you – Royal Navy Stripey – 85 piastres."

He wasn't looking quite so cocky now, we thought. Perhaps he was thinking, 'Old Stripey is not so stupid after all.'

Anyway, after a few more minutes' haggling they settled on 75 piastres.

"Get them down near to the price you are prepared to pay, Stripey had told us, then start to walk out. That will bring them round!"

"All right, all right, Jack – 75 piastres."

You walk out with your purchase, pleased as Punch, thinking you have put one over on him; and he probably stands there grinning his head off, knowing that he had you.

I guess I must have finally dozed off; I was awakened by something knocking against my shoulder, and a voice shouting at me. I opened my eyes and vaguely realised it was Petty Officer Simpson's voice, and his knee knocking against my shoulder.

"Wakey-wakey! Let's be having you, then," he shouted.

I was still only half awake, but another blast from the Petty Officer soon remedied that.

"Come on, then – on your feet! This isn't a bloody pleasure cruise!"

Even as he spoke, there was the sound of gunfire.

"Torpedo bombers, Matt," said Taff as I jumped up.

He and I worked as a team, loading and making up belts for the pom-poms, and drums for the Oerlikons.

I caught a glimpse of several planes, low down, some distance out beyond the destroyer screen. Our own guns were silent, as there was a real danger of ships hitting one another when firing at low-flying aircraft. There was a real danger also of ships colliding when they made emergency turns to avoid torpedoes. After the torpedo bombers, came the high-level ones, and then the Stuka dive-bombers. We were subjected to near-continuous attacks for most of the afternoon, but, by what could only have been a miracle, none of the ships were hit – none directly, that is, but all received splinter damage and casualties from many near misses.

Seven attackers were brought down. Our pom-pom crew claimed a dive-bomber. The Stukas made an awful screaming noise when they came down at us – we heard it quite clearly over the deafening racket of the gunfire.

They would form up in a rough circle above the ships, then

84

peel off, one after another, and choose their individual targets.

I stole a glance up over my shoulder during one attack, and watched fascinated as the all too familiar black-painted W shape came hurtling down – straight at me personally, it seemed.

The noise of the barrage going up was deafening, in spite of our earplugs. Our ten 5.25s were firing almost directly overhead. The crash each time a gun was fired felt like a blow on the head. Then came the 'thump, thump, thump' of the pom-poms as they opened up, then the twenty-millimetre Oerlikons, and finally the quadruple .5s. They made an ear-splitting crackling noise.

Empty shell cases were cascading down off the gun mounting, rolling around the deck in all directions, and getting under our feet. There seemed to be hundreds of them.

"I haven't been skating for years," Steve shouted in my ear as he scooped up another belt of ammunition.

"Spare hand, grab a broom," roared Petty Officer Simpson. "Get rid of them – over the side – anywhere!"

I saw the bomb released, and, holding my breath, turned my attention back to the Oerlikon drum we were reloading. The deck began to tilt as we made an emergency turn, and then came the crash of the explosion.

A great column of water rose close alongside and seemed to hang there for a few seconds; then, as it descended, a curtain of spray swept across the gun deck.

'Hell!' I thought. 'That was mighty close. I hope we are all right.'

"Lovely Mediterranean cruises!" shouted Steve, as he stood there soaking wet. "Free shower baths thrown in!"

That near miss was one of many during the afternoon. A war correspondent we had with us recorded some ninety in a four-hour period, from dive-bombers and high-level bombers.

The expenditure of ammunition was colossal in these attacks, out of all proportion to the number of aircraft destroyed, but it served the purpose of putting them off their aim – or so we hoped.

Five men were injured by splinters during the attacks, but

none mortally, we learned later. One member of the port-side pom-pom crew received a splinter high in the chest, and it passed out through the shoulder. One of the Oerlikon gunners just astern of our position had the two middle fingers of one hand carried away.

The attacks gradually petered out in the early evening, much to our relief, but meanwhile other things were happening. The four cruisers had increased speed and were roaring ahead. Signal lamps were flashing between them.

Presently we altered course more to the northward, while the destroyers closed in, formed a close screen around the single ship we were escorting, and turned away to the south.

The gun communication number spoke to Petty Officer Simpson, and handed him the headset.

"What the hell is going on?" someone asked. I think we were all wondering the same thing.

We were enlightened a couple of minutes later when four huge plumes of water rose about 300 yards off our starboard beam.

We looked at each other in disbelief – there was no sound of aircraft engines.

"Oh, my Gawd!" said Ginger. "Battlers [battleships]! The bleeding Italian Fleet is up ahead!"

Our three forward turrets suddenly opened up, and black smoke began pouring from the funnels.

Petty Officer Simpson addressed us: "Pay attention, lads. There are two Italian battleships and some heavy cruisers up ahead. We have got to hold them off until the convoy gets clear."

"Oh no!" said Steve. "Why did I ever decide to join the navy!" He turned towards the bridge, looked up and shouted. "We all know you are mad, but you ain't going to tackle that lot, surely."

We called our captain 'the Mad Admiral'. He wasn't that, but he was a brilliant and fearless leader, and he was already a household name back home for a daring exploit earlier in the war. As a destroyer captain, he had captured and boarded a German prison ship, and freed a number of Royal Navy and merchant-navy men.

He had joined us quite recently, and this present operation was his third trip, as far as I remember. He was to attain the very highest rank in the service eventually.

More Italian shells fell – not quite so close this time, fortunately for us.

"Those fifteen-inch projees weigh one ton each," Petty Officer Simpson remarked. "If one of those bastards falls on us, I reckon it will go straight down and out through the bottom of the ship!"

There was, by now, a dense smokescreen between us, but we learned that the enemy ships had turned away to the north. Our four cruisers turned away to the south-west at high speed to catch up with the convoy.

Standing on the boom deck, facing aft, I watched as 'X' and 'Y' turrets fired a few parting shots in the direction of the enemy. Darkness was gathering, and we saw red streaks in the sky as the shells sped away.

As the war in the desert ebbed and flowed, so it affected our convoy to Malta. When the Afrika Korps drove our armies back to the Egyptian frontier, the convoys had to be suspended for a time, as it became too costly to run them.

The last one we attempted was a total disaster. The Germans now had airfields on three sides of us at Sicily, Crete and now Cyrenaica, and the few squadrons of fighters we had in the desert had to be withdrawn to Egypt.

It had become too risky to keep an aircraft carrier on the station – two we had with us earlier had been seriously damaged, and they had to be withdrawn. It was the beginning of an unhappy period for the navy.

The convoy I just mentioned was bombed without mercy, and all three ships we were escorting were lost, together with their vital supplies. Two of them, burning fiercely after dive-bombing attacks, had to be sunk by our own forces. We returned to Alexandria in very low spirits.

We put to sea again the next day, when it was reported that units of the Italian Fleet were at sea. Our three battleships, with their destroyer screen, also sailed. No enemy ships were encountered, but disaster befell us again. The battleship *Barham* was lost. Hit by three torpedoes from a U-boat, she rolled over on to her side, and blew up. More than half her complement of over 1,000 men lost their lives.

Many of my old classmates at *Ganges* had been drafted to the *Barham*, I learned later.

A fortnight or so after this sad event, we lost one of the ships of our own squadron – the cruiser *Galatea*. The squadron was about to enter the swept channel just outside Alexandria Harbour, returning from another fruitless search for enemy ships. She was hit by two torpedoes, and sank almost at once, with heavy loss of life. We were very saddened by this loss – the four cruisers had been a very efficient unit.

To cap it all, we were to have our two remaining battleships put out of action a few days later. Italian frogmen, in a daring exploit, got into the harbour when the boom defence was opened for some of our ships to enter, and attached limpet mines to their keels. They exploded early the following morning, and blew large holes in the bottoms of both ships. They settled on the harbour bottom, and were out of action for several months while temporary repairs were carried out.

Command of the Eastern Mediterranean now rested with the three remaining ships of 15th Cruiser Squadron and a handful of destroyers.

"If the Italian Fleet shows its hand now," said one thoughtful character, "I reckon we're done for!"

Thankfully, it didn't.

Most of our troubles on the Malta convoys had been due to the lack of fighter aircraft cover. It was not the fault of the RAF – they just did not have the planes available. The few Spitfires and Hurricanes did not have the range to escort us very far from their bases, and, of course, as their bases were pushed back, as the desert war see-sawed, the cover became less and less. A few squadrons of long-range fighters would have saved us some headaches, I think, not to mention men's lives, ships and ammunition.

I remember one of the petty officers telling me after one trip we did that our ship alone had fired over 1,000 rounds of 5.25 ammunition.

Members of the Seaman Branch of the navy were jacks of all trades, whereas members of the Stoker Branch were concerned only with the engine, boiler rooms and various auxiliary machinery. Members of the Signal Branch were concerned with their flags and signal lamps, the telegraphists with their radios, but the seamen carried out all kinds of duties, including cleaning and painting the ship, and such things as mooring, splicing ropes and wires, forming boats' crews, shore patrols and boarding parties, and acting as sentries.

When you qualified as an able seaman, you were then channelled into one of four directions: gunnery, torpedo, radar or asdic. This decided your non-substantive rating, for which you received extra pay.

I had been seriously thinking of putting in for a gunnery course – I wanted to have a go at those dive-bombers! I had grown up, so to speak, with guns of various kinds, and had become quite a reasonable shot. There was a miniature rifle range (.22) in Chatham Barracks, and I spent many sessions there. Sixpence for five rounds, I believe, was the charge.

"What, you again!" the attendant would greet me.

I knocked the centre right out of a good many targets in Chatham Barracks.

Perhaps I had got my shooting ability from my father. Not many things escaped when he pointed his gun at them – rats, rabbits and pigeons (and other unmentionable creatures sometimes). Father had served in the regular army – cavalry, actually – before, and throughout, the First World War.

A little story comes to mind, which he told several times when we were children. He was a member of the team representing his regiment in the army .303 championships, apparently, a year or so before the war broke out.

"I was the last man to shoot," he said, "and our team needed not less than three bulls and two inners with five rounds to win the championship, and that was exactly what I got."

As I said, I was thinking of putting in for a gunnery course, and one month and two more convoys to Malta later the matter was decided for me. It seemed another theatre, and a different sort of war, was beckoning.

Six of us were piped to report to the coxswain's office, the day after we arrived back. The coxswain was the senior seaman chief petty officer on our ship. One of his duties was arranging the transfer of men, although at the time I don't think any of us thought that anything like that was in the offing.

We stood there in front of his desk, waiting and wondering, while he shuffled through some papers, which he then placed in a neat little pile to one side.

"Right then, lads – are we all here?" he asked as he looked up.

"Yes, Chief." And we gave our names.

Looking at each of us in turn, he smiled and said, "You are not in the rattle, so there's no need to look so bloody miserable. I have got good news for you: this is your lucky day. You are going home!"

Going home? Had he really said that, or was I dreaming?

I collected my wits as he began talking again: "Things seem to be going pretty bad for us in the Atlantic. U-boats are sinking our ships bloody wholesale, by the sound of it! You lads are being drafted back to the UK for training as submarine detector operators. More lads are coming off the other ships as well, so there will be quite a sizeable party of you going. I can't tell you any more than that, except to say you will all get a nice bit of foreign-service leave when you arrive. Get your gear packed ready, and listen for the pipes – OK?"

I felt I was walking on air when I left his office to go back to my mess. I still couldn't quite believe it – had I really been reprieved? Probably like all the other lads, I had become convinced that I would never be going home again. One day, I thought, somewhere between Alexandria and Malta, we would all go to our graves.

After the best part of the year on the station, I was beginning to feel rather low. Lack of proper sleep for days at a time, and being continually tensed up, was taking its toll. My messmates gave me some stick when I told them I was going.

"Lucky bastard!", "Bloody creep!", "Snivelling bleeder!" and "Deserter!" were some of the comments.

It goes without saying I was pleased and thankful to get away, and yet I was sad at the same time, especially when saying goodbye to my special mates in the pom-pom crew.

"Wish we were coming with you, Matt," said Steve as we shook hands.

"I wish you were too," I replied.

I was sad for another reason also. My brother Arthur was in the desert with 33 Squadron (Spitfires), and he had tried to get on my ship a couple of times when he had a few hours' leave in Alexandria, but unfortunately we had been at sea on both occasions. However, several weeks later he did make it at the third attempt, and I was to be grateful for that.

Oddly enough, my mess number on the ship was the same as his squadron number: 33.

I wrote a last letter home to let my parents know I was leaving the ship, and, later the same day, our little party was put ashore.

The ship that took us on the first stage of the journey home didn't compare with the two I had come out on. Obviously very old, she was pretty scruffy generally. Below decks, paint was flaking off the bulkheads, ventilation was poor and there were cockroaches everywhere. She was probably rescued from the breaker's yard, suggested someone. Never mind, we thought. As long as she stays afloat, we don't care what condition she's in. We were on our way home – that was the most important thing.

It was great really, after what we had been through, in spite of the poor conditions. I was beginning to feel considerably more cheerful already, and I hadn't seen so many happy faces for a long time. There were no watch-keeping duties, no action stations and no dive-bombers, and we were not living on our nerves any more.

We had a little bit of excitement on about the fourth or fifth day. The ship was carrying several hundred German and Italian prisoners of war, including Rommel's second in command, in addition to the naval draft and other military personnel. It was discovered that prisoners were fashioning various kinds of weapons and planned to seize the ship. It caused a bit of a flap for a time. All available firearms were issued out – those that didn't get one armed themselves with a suitable wooden club!

The captain in charge of the troops guarding the prisoners said to us, "I trust the navy will give a good account of itself if anything happens."

He needn't have worried – nothing did. A party of the toughest-looking troops went below, guns at the ready, and sorted the ringleaders out; and that was the end of it.

Several more leisurely days passed, and we arrived at Durban, where we disembarked and were taken to a tented camp a mile or two outside the city. We would be spending two weeks here, we were informed. This didn't go down too well as we were impatient to get home – most of us, anyway.

"I don't know what you lot are moaning about," remarked one chap. "We have got it made here, if you think about it. The routine is dead easy, not a bit pusser, lashings of good grub, lovely climate, plenty of booze and skirt in town and the bleeding war is 1,000 miles away. They can leave me here till it ends if they like!"

"I reckon he's scared to go home," said a voice: "scared he might find a bloody pongo in his bed."

I remember that stay at Durban for three things.

The first was a visit to the snake park. I'm not all that fond of snakes – I don't suppose many other folk are either – but it was quite an education. An attendant strolled round with us, explaining about the different species, their habitats and diets, etc. Just inside the entrance gates was a large evergreen bush, and when we were invited to examine it at close quarters we found it to be absolutely alive with snakes. We took a hasty step or two back.

"Don't be alarmed," said the attendant. "They are all quite harmless."

He reached in, picked one up and offered it to the chap standing next to me.

"I don't think I'll bother," he said.

All the dangerous ones were in cages and enclosures, behind plate glass. We saw huge boa constrictors and pythons, and a large pool in the centre of the park contained many water snakes. It was well worth the visit, I thought.

My second memory is of seeing the battleship *Nelson* at close quarters. It was the day before we sailed on the next stage of the journey home. We had boarded the ship that was to take us back that morning – a more modern ship, this one. She looked very clean and comfortable – a liner of about 20,000 tons.

During the afternoon, there was an announcement over the Tannoy: "For anyone interested, the battleship *Nelson* is about to pass down the port side."

I dashed up top, and watched as she passed slowly by, heading for her berth. I had seen her once or twice before, but only at a distance. We were all well genned up on aircraft and ship recognition, and there was no mistaking that long forecastle, with its three massive sixteen-inch turrets.

"Cor!" muttered someone. "Look at those bloody great guns!"

"What do you reckon each of those weigh?" asked the chief petty officer in charge of our draft as he joined us at the rail.

"No idea," someone replied.

"Have a guess," said the Chief.

"Ten tons" from one lad; "Twenty tons" from another; "Forty tons," said a third voice.

"You are a long way out," said the Chief. "Each of those guns weighs 103.5 tons."

"Bloody hell!" someone exclaimed.

He told us much more about the *Nelson* – details of her construction and layout, etc., and I for one was quite fascinated listening to him. Apparently he had spent three years on her sister ship, *Rodney*, in the thirties.

My third memory of Durban on this occasion is a very sad

one. It was on the following morning I heard the news that a small party of late arrivals had come on board, brought down from Suez in a destroyer.

We were standing chatting together when one of them asked if any of our party had been on the cruiser flagship. When I replied that I had, he said, "Well, you got off just in time, mate – she has been sunk."

'Oh no!' I thought. 'Ginger, Steve, old Stripey, Gordon, and all the others!'

"Casualties?" I hardly dared ask the question.

"I don't know, mate," he replied. "I can't tell you any more. Sorry," he added.

Apparently, she had sailed again for Malta a few days after our little party had left, and was sunk by a U-boat. I kept wondering how many men had gone down with her. I hoped it was not too many.

We sailed a few hours later for Cape Town, where we spent one day, then on up to Freetown. On the way we had a practice shoot. Two crews had been formed for watch-keeping on the six-inch gun mounted aft, and we fired ten or twelve rounds at a large wooden crate which had been dropped overboard. We changed round positions on the gun for each shot, which gave several of us experience at pulling the trigger. We didn't hit the crate, but several of the shots were fairly close.

At Freetown we joined up with a convoy – homeward bound, destination Liverpool.

CHAPTER 7

BONNIE SCOTLAND (I): REST CURE

The Petty Officer submarine detector instructor (SDI) addressed the class: "Can you all hear me?" he asked.

There was a chorus of "Yes" in reply.

"Now, why can you hear me – leaving aside the fact that you have got ears?"

There was complete silence from the class.

"I will tell you why you can hear me," he went on. "It's because my voice is sending out sound waves." He picked up a small bell and tapped it with a pencil; then he tapped a tuning fork on the edge of the table. "Can you hear those?" he asked.

There was a chorus of "Yes" from the class.

SDI: Why could you hear them?

CLASS: Because they were sending out sound waves.

SDI: They were sending out sound waves because they were made to vibrate. When we speak, we vibrate our vocal chords. If we pluck a guitar string, the same thing happens. So far so good. We have established the fact that anything that vibrates sends out sound waves. We will now establish something else: these sound waves we have mentioned, and all others from normal sources, are of a very low frequency and consequently travel out in all directions. Are you with me?

CLASS: Yes.

SDI: Now, asdic transmission is of a very high frequency – in the region of twenty kilohertz – 20,000 complete vibrations per second. Being such a high frequency, these sound waves are concentrated into a very narrow beam. Are you all happy so far?

CLASS: Yes.

SDI: We will move on a stage further now. Echoes – what do we know about echoes?

Several hands were raised, and examples were given of places where you might expect to hear echoes.

"Good," said the SDI. "We have now established something else: sound waves striking something solid will be reflected back in the form of echoes. Very high-frequency sound waves going out in a narrow beam underwater and striking a submarine will give us back echoes. Now," he continued, "if we know the speed these sound waves travel at, we can work out how far away the submarine is, using the time taken for the transmission going out and the echoes coming back. We do know", he went on, "that the speed of sound through the atmosphere is 750 feet per second, and through seawater is 5,000 feet per second."

'This all sounds very interesting,' I thought.

There was a pleasant and friendly atmosphere and only a relatively small number of people. What a contrast to Chatham Barracks and the hell of those Malta convoys!

"We will pause a moment" – the SDI's voice came through to me – "until our friend in the second row has finished his daydreams!"

"Sorry, SDI," I said. "I was thinking about what you were saying."

We had a general discussion, and a question-and-answer session. One thing in particular I had been wondering about, and asked him: "What makes the transmission signal such a high frequency?"

"Twenty thousand volts," he replied. "But more about that tomorrow."

It was the end of instruction for the day. I found it very interesting. I was looking forward to learning more.

Upon the outbreak of war, it was decided to transfer the anti-submarine training school and headquarters away from the south coast, to where it would be less vulnerable to German air attacks. It was known as HMS *Nimrod/Osprey*. *Nimrod,* the basic training section, went to a small coastal town in Western Scotland, and *Osprey*, the headquarters and disposal base, went to a place a little further up the coast.

We had arrived at the former the previous day, after spending a month in Chatham Barracks and three weeks at home on foreign-service leave.

The journey up had been very enjoyable – the very fact we were getting away from Chatham was a tonic in itself. What a depressing place Chatham was!

It seemed so peaceful and quiet up here and there was lovely sunny weather and grand scenery. The war could be almost forgotten.

HMS *Nimrod* was housed in what had formerly been a school. A certain amount of conversion work had taken place, and asdic equipment had been installed. Although basic naval routine was observed, the general atmosphere was very relaxed.

I was looking forward to going ashore and having a good walk around. (We used the term 'going ashore', whether based on a ship or in a shore establishment.)

A number of small vessels fitted out with asdic sets were attached to the base, together with a 'friendly' submarine for our sea training. As a matter of interest, one of the former was Sir Bernard Docker's luxury yacht, the *Shemara*. She had been commandeered by the navy, as had many other small vessels, for military use. I spent several hours at her wheel, in between sessions operating the asdic set.

Our second day's instruction had begun. Our instructor said, "First of all, lads, it might be a good idea if I told you what A.S.D.I.C. stands for: Allied Submarine Detection Investigation Committee – nowadays they call it sonar. Oscillators," he continued: "an oscillator is something that vibrates, and so sends out sound waves. The asdic oscillator is round in shape, has a diameter of twenty inches, and is about nine inches thick. It is constructed of alternate stainless-steel and quartz plates, and the unit is enclosed in a steel shell – the front face being left open. The complete unit weighs one and a half hundredweight. The oscillator, on its shaft, is suspended below the ship's bottom inside a streamlined dome, which has a stainless-steel shell and a watertight fitting to the ship's bottom. On slow ships, such as sloops, frigates and corvettes, etc., the dome is a rigid fixture, while on faster ships, such as destroyers, the dome with its oscillator is retractable, the reason being that it could be damaged or even carried away at high speed. Everyone happy so far?" he asked.

A chorus of "Yes" came from the class.

He continued: "At the upper end of the oscillator shaft, inside the ship, is the electrical connection and traversing gear. I will describe briefly the remaining components of the set, and tomorrow you will be seeing it all in the PTH. The components are power supply, transmitter, receiver, range and bearing recorders, traversing control gear, and earphones. There is also, of course, a gyrocompass repeater – we need to know what bearing our oscillator is pointing on, don't we? By the way," he continued, "the control gear and operators are usually housed in a cabouche up on the bridge, but it can be placed elsewhere in the ship if necessary."

We had another question-and-answer session, and then it was 'stand easy'.

We sat outside in the sun – a small party of us, smoking and chatting.

"Home from home this," one lad remarked. "How long is this course – six weeks? I wish it was six months!"

"It's like being on holiday," said Tommo, a close friend of mine. "A real rest cure!" he added.

"Some contrast from Chatham Barracks," I said. "I wonder what all those poor devils are doing now."

"Area bloody sweeping, I expect," said one of the others. "Remember that area sweeping? Spend all the bleeding morning sweeping your patch, even though there was nothing to pick up! What was the point of it, I would like to know?"

"They were keeping you occupied," said Tommo.

"I wish they had let me go out for a bloody good walk. It would have done me more good, I should think."

"They wouldn't do that in case you kept on walking," said Nick Carter. "I never felt so miserable in my whole life before," he added. "I must be a lunatic to say it, but I honestly wished I was back in the Med on those Malta convoys!"

"I know what you mean, Nick," I said. "I felt something like that myself."

Nick and I had travelled back to the UK together, and I learned he had been on one of the cruisers in my group.

"That Gestapo lot got me down," one lad remarked. "Them bastards hounded us from pillar to post – weren't safe to load anywhere for more than a couple of minutes. They lumbered me in the sickbay one morning," he went on.

"What was you there for, Stan?" asked Nick. "Caught the boat up, had you?"

"No, course not," was the reply. "I take precautions, don't I? Nothing like that," he said. "I was having a quiet little loaf – minding my own business, so to speak. I'd been there a few times – you just needed to watch the sickbay tiffy didn't hustle you in before the quack before you realised what was happening!"

"Anyway, this particular morning there was a whole crowd of blokes there. I don't know how many of them were sick, or just loafing like me, but, anyway, I got myself in a corner with four or five others and was watching points, so to speak. The sickbay tiffy kept poking his head round the door, shouting, 'Next!' Well, after a bit he comes through into the waiting room, and across to where our little group was sat.

"'Hello,' I thought. 'What are you up to, then? What's your game?'

"Well, he stops about six feet away from us – didn't seem as though he wanted to come too close – sneers, looks down his nose and says, 'Right then, you dirty lot of bleeders what have got crabs, get down to the bathroom a bit sharpish, and get shaved off!'

"'Bloody hell!' I thought. 'I ain't got crabs – I've got to get out of here pretty sharpish!'"

We were all becoming highly amused by now.

"You probably had got crabs by then, Stan," said Tommo, "especially if you were sitting close to them."

"Go on, Stan – tell us what happened next," I said.

"Well, as soon as that tiffy turned his back, I was off the chair like greased lightning and making for the door. Then I spotted them."

"Spotted who?" someone asked.

"Why – the Gestapo," Stan replied, "two of the bleeders. They must have sneaked in quiet, like, and planted themselves by the door."

"What happened then, Stan? What did you do?"

"What did I do? Couldn't do anything, could I? The game was up, wasn't it? I came to a sudden stop, and stood there looking a prize bloody idiot, I should think.

"One of the bleeders looked at the other and said, 'This one seems to have made a speedy recovery!' Then he looks at me with a spiteful little grin on his face, and says, 'What's your trouble, then?'

"'I ain't got no trouble,' I answered.

"'Well, I reckon you have,' he replied. 'You've got trouble if you're sick, and a lot more trouble if you ain't!'"

Our little group were laughing our heads off by now.

"It must be nearly time for out pipes," said Nick. "Tell us quick what happened, Stan."

"I was going to, till you butted in," Stan replied.

"Well, the other bleeder looks at me and says, 'What's the matter with you, then? What disease or complaint are you suffering from?'

"'None,' I told him.

"'Ho ho,' he sneered. 'Mind telling us what you are doing here, then?'

"'Loafing,' I answered.

"Well, the bastard turned to his mate and said in a sarcastic little voice, 'At least he's an honest loafer, ain't he? What are we going to do with him?'

"I thought I might have got off," said Stan, "but the bastard turned back to me, and says, 'First Lieutenant's report – let's have your station card!'"

"You thought you might have got off!" said Tommo. "You had just told them you were loafing – you must be a bloody imbecile!"

"Well, I tried," said Stan. "I thought if I told them the truth, they might call it extensive circumstances – or something like that," he added.

"You mean extenuating circumstances," said Nick. "You're a bloody lunatic, Stan!"

"How did you get on, Stan?" I asked.

"Oh, the usual," he replied: "a few days' stoppage of leave."

"Hi, you lot!" One of our classmates was shouting from the corner of a nearby building.

"What's the matter with him?" someone said.

"What do you want?" called Nick.

"I don't want anything," came the reply, "but the SDI wants you lot back in the classroom. Out pipes went nearly five minutes ago – he ain't very pleased, I can tell you."

"Bloody hell!" said Tommo. "None of us heard it."

We jumped up, dashed inside and took our seats – all feeling and looking, I should imagine, a bit sheepish.

"What happened to you lot?" asked the SDI. "Did you lose your bearings or doze off in the sun? Or have you all gone stone deaf?"

There was silence from us.

"Perhaps we had better get your ears syringed. As a matter of interest," he continued, "you'll have that done at regular intervals. You don't want to have your ears bunged up with muck stopping those echoes getting in, do you? It's quite painless," he went on, "so don't try to dodge it. You wouldn't want to find yourself swimming in the middle of the Atlantic, and thinking, 'If I had had my ears done like I should have, I might have detected that bloody U-boat!' Right then, lads – back to business! Now, where did we get to?" He looked directly at me.

"You mentioned reverberations," I replied.

"Reverberations!" He repeated the word. "In an electrical storm we see the flash of powerful electric currents. In the resulting explosion, sound waves are sent out, and we hear the rumble of thunder. These are reverberations – the sound waves bouncing back and forth among the clouds. When we send out an asdic transmission we hear many reverberations – from shoals of fish, from plankton, from larger individual fish, from layers of water of different temperatures or density, from tide rips and eddies, etc., etc. Am I getting through?" he asked.

There was a chorus of "Yes" again.

He continued: "I imagine you are all saying to yourselves, 'How the hell are we going to pick out a U-boat echo from amongst that lot!' Thankfully," he went on, "there are some things to help us. Small echoes, such as those I have just mentioned, will not be very sharp and clear. We could describe them as being 'woolly' – also they may cover a wide extent of bearing, whereas a U-boat certainly will not. For example, we would not expect an echo from a U-boat at, say, 2,000 yards, to be more than three or four degrees in extent. One more thing to assist us is the Doppler effect." He looked around the class, and repeated the word. "Doppler. Can anyone tell me what is meant by Doppler?"

There was silence from the class.

"I don't suppose you would know, lads, because you haven't been told. Doppler is echo pitch. Let us imagine we are out in the Atlantic on convoy escort duties. We have obtained an echo, quite sharp and clear – we are not quite convinced, and have classified it as doubtful. We need more information. We check the extent of bearing in relation to the range, and whether there is any echo pitch (Doppler). If we can establish that the former is quite small, and the echo pitch is a higher or lower note than the transmission, then we can be pretty sure we are in contact with a U-boat, and we report it as such. The Doppler will also tell us whether the U-boat is coming towards us or going away, at a slight, moderate or marked angle – echo slight, moderate, or marked, high or low, as the case may be. Now, on the other hand, if the U-boat is lying stopped, or travelling on a parallel course to ours, there will be no Doppler effect – so, as you can see, there will be plenty to think about. By the way," he went on,

"I omitted to tell you that echoes will also be obtained from surface vessels, but, of course, the bridge staff and lookouts check the bearing and distance, and where they coincide with the position of a surface vessel you will be told to disregard." The SDI's manner changed slightly now. "I want to impress upon you all that whether a convoy or individual ships of a convoy reach their destination safely will depend on your abilities and dedication as asdic operators. When you are out there operating the set, you will be doing the most important job on the ship; and when you detect a U-boat, your captain will be relying on the information you give him to enable him to make a successful attack."

We had another short question-and-answer section, and then it was dinner time.

I had arranged to go ashore later in the afternoon with Tommo, and have a look around. Harry Thomas was his full name, and he was from Nottingham, about the same age as myself. We had become good mates.

Dinner break ended, and it was out pipes and back to school.

"Everybody here?" the SDI asked.

There was a mumbled reply from the class.

"Good – we will talk about hydrophones, and hydrophone effect. Not only is the oscillator a transmitter/receiver, it is also a hydrophone, or underwater microphone. We can stop transmitting and just listen to the natural sounds of the sea. Whistling, crackling and clicking may be the noises of various kinds of fish. We also hear the sounds of ships' engines and propellers, and sadly, sometimes, ships breaking up as they go down. Speaking of ships' propellers," he continued, "you will soon learn the difference between the various kinds of propulsion – reciprocating engines, turbines and diesels. The sounds are quite different. You'll be hearing them on tape in the PTH."

The remainder of the session was taken up with a general discussion, and I for one was finding the course quite fascinating. This was a completely new field for me – so different from normal seamanship duties, and the procedures associated with various types of guns and gunnery. In contrast with other instructors, as Tommo had remarked, the SDI was quite a normal and likeable human being – which is more than could be said of some of the chief gunners' mates!

"I think all of us asdic types are more genteel," said Stan.

We thought that observation was a bit amusing, coming from him (he was a bit on the uncouth side).

"What do you reckon to it all?" Tommo asked as we left the base.

"I like it," I replied, "but there is a lot more to it than I thought. I had no idea really."

"I didn't either, Matt, but I like it too. I think it was our lucky day when they picked our names out. This place is dead easy – not a bit pusser. I was wondering – when we finish our course, do we go straight to the ship from here?"

"No, Tommo," I replied. "I was chatting to one of the blokes from the other class, and he told me we get a long weekend's leave at the end of the course, and then come back to the headquarters depot for disposal. It's up the coast a bit from here, I believe, but I don't know where exactly. That will be our base for the remainder of the war."

"I wonder how long we will be there before we get a ship, Matt – I hope we get the same one."

"So do I, Tommo," I replied, "but I reckon we will be mighty lucky if we do. I wonder what it is like out there in the Atlantic. I shall miss that Mediterranean sunshine!"

"Yes," he replied, "but at least there won't be any dive-bombers. I wonder if many of the convoy escorts get sunk by U-boats?"

"I don't know," I said, "but I should imagine they are more interested in the merchant packets."

"Things aren't going too well for us, Matt, according to what the SDI was saying. No end of our merchant ships are going down – he reckons they are sinking them faster than we can build them."

"Yes, I remember what they told us when we arrived here," I said: "the situation in the Atlantic had reached a critical stage, and there was a crying need for more escort vessels and asdic operators. I guess we shall find out, Tommo, what it's all about."

"I wonder how far it is across to the mainland," Tommo remarked. "I've no idea," I replied. "When we get back to the base, Tommo, we'll borrow a chart so we can check on the whole area. I have been looking at that big rock out there – we can check on that also."

"Do you reckon it has got a name, Matt?"

"Sure to have," I replied. "I wonder how far it is from here?"

"Difficult to judge, Matt. Distance over water is very deceiving. It could be anything from ten to twenty miles – maybe more."

We had climbed some considerable distance up in the hills on the outskirts of town, and were sat on a grassy bank overlooking the Firth. The town lay down to our left. In its harbour several small boats lay at anchor or moored to buoys. A little way out on the south side of the harbour was a small island with a lighthouse. It was a picturesque scene, and very peaceful.

"I could quite easily spend the rest of the war sitting here," Tommo remarked.

We sat at that spot several times during our walks in the hills. I didn't know it then, but across the Firth, over beyond that lonely rock, in a small hamlet on the mainland there lived someone I was to meet about two and half years later – someone I was to spend many happy hours with, and who became rather special.

Checking on a map some years later, I found that her home was almost directly across from where Tommo and I used to sit. Considering the large area of Scotland, and all its towns and villages, it is quite remarkable that her house happened to be just there.

"The range of the asdic transmission is a very interesting matter," remarked the SDI. "Normally, at sea on convoy duty, we transmit to a range of 2,500 yards. What I mean by that is the transmission interval is timed to permit any echo to be received from the range before it is drowned out by the noise of the next transmission. The sound waves will still carry on for quite some distance, but of course getting weaker all the time. Am I making sense?" he asked.

There were murmurs from the class in reply.

"It is possible", he continued, "for echoes to be obtained from much further afield if we allow a longer interval between transmissions, but the danger here is that a U-boat could slip through the screen undetected. Two thousand five hundred yards is reckoned to be ideal, and of course at this distance the escort vessels' sweeps overlap. The ships in each group have a different frequency set, to avoid interference with one another. Incorporated in the asdic set is a Morse key, which enables us to make single transmissions. Now, under ideal conditions it is possible to get echoes from perhaps 10,000 or 12,000 yards. To get the range when using the Morse key", he added, "we use a stopwatch. Escort vessels can also communicate with each other using the Morse code – provided their operators know it! The sets need to be using the same frequency. As a matter of interest, I personally have obtained echoes at about 9,000 yards while lying in a sheltered anchorage."

Our first few days were spent absorbing the theory of it all; then we began intensive training in the Procedure and Attack teaching huts. Most of us – all of us – made a complete hash of things to begin with. It was all so different. Holding on to that elusive echo when we got a contact in the search/sweep simulator needed great concentration. Listening intently to any change in Doppler and observing alterations in position, we were all the time making reports on the range and bearing.

After a few days of this, we began sea training with a friendly submarine (clockwork mouse, we called it). We gradually became more proficient at holding the contact, once we had found it, in spite of the varied manoeuvres it adopted in trying to escape – round and round in circles perhaps, first one way and then the other. Then we would make a mock attack, the results being analysed afterwards.

We were given a reactions test towards the end of the course, which again was analysed. Quite hilarious this test was at times.

We sat at a desk, with four button switches in front of us, labelled in turn, 'Bell', 'Lamp', 'High Note Buzzer', and 'Low Note Buzzer'. The idea was to stab the appropriate button as quickly as possible when the lamp flashed, the bell rang or either of the buzzers sounded. This did not occur in a regular sequence – they came at random, quite fast, and with hopeless results in some cases!

We were all rather sad when the course ended as it had been a very welcome break in a pleasant atmosphere and lovely surroundings – a holiday almost.

I had a nice surprise for my family when I arrived home for the weekend.

The canteen manager called round at the mess just before I left, late on the Friday morning.

"Your lot have not collected their nutty [chocolate] rationing," he said. "Don't they want it?"

"They have all gone off for the weekend," I said. "I'm going myself in a few minutes."

"Well, it's there in the canteen, chum. If you'd like to pay for it, you can have the whole bleeding lot as far as I'm concerned!"

I did just that.

I rejoined my mates on the bus that took us to the little ferry terminal some distance up the coast. All were greatly excited about going home for the weekend – I think they had forgotten all about chocolate; there were other things on their minds, no doubt.

The trip on the ferry was most enjoyable. It was a beautiful sunny day, and we called at Ardrishaig, Tighnabruaich and Rothesay, on our way to Wemyss Bay, where we caught a train for Glasgow.

I was looking forward to going home, yet sad to be leaving.

CHAPTER 8

ATLANTIC CONVOYS

She was the senior ship of an Atlantic escort group, a sloop of
about 1,100 tons displacement, with a complement of 150 men.
My first ship had also been the senior ship of the group – flagship
of 15th Cruiser Squadron, but I doubted if this one would have
a rear admiral on board.

This escort group's number seemed to remind me of
something, and after a while it came to me: it was the same as
the number of a fire-watcher party I had been a member of in
Chatham Barracks.

I was sitting in Moony's Bar, Belfast, with some of my
new shipmates. George Weaver and I had joined her the
previous day, coming from HMS *Osprey*, the asdic
headquarters base.

I had spent a very enjoyable long weekend at home after
completing the training course, and then I made the long
journey back up to Scotland, to HMS *Osprey*, for disposal.

George and I had been in the same mess at the base, and I
was pleased that we had been drafted to the same ship. It was
nice to have at least one person I knew. A Londoner, his
peacetime occupation had been bookmaker's runner and tic-
tac man – among other things. George had been acquainted
with a good number of odd characters, I think, judging by the
stories he told me.

"I've left Newmarket Racecourse more than once in a hell
of a hurry with the guv'nor!"

We heard stories of hair-raising escapades, some relating to jewellers' shop windows.

"All that was needed", he said, "was a sheet of brown paper, a tin of treacle and half a house brick!"

I had liked the little ship straight away. Sloops were quite roomy – plenty of space on the mess decks – and they were good sea boats, I was told. She had a four-inch gun forward and aft, and a few twenty-millimetre Oerlikons, but her primary armaments, of course, were the asdic and depth charges.

The asdic operating gear was up on the bridge, in a cosy little cabouche. The set was a type 127, but we were informed that one of the newer type (144) was to be fitted at the next refit. The basic principle and procedure was exactly the same, but the 144 was much more sophisticated, in that it had automatic sweep, bearing and depth recorders.

During the remainder of our stay at Belfast I got to know my fellow operators. There were six of us, and we would be working in pairs, we learned. Only one of our party was a naval regular; the remainder, like me, were 'hostilities only'.

Ted Stevens was a Birmingham lad, shrewd and talkative – similar to George Weaver. The two of them soon formed a friendship, and became watch-keeping partners. Stan Gilligan, a Geordie, teamed up with Jim Kirby, another North Country lad, and my own watch-keeping partner was 'Jock' Bob Munro, who before the war had been a surveyor. Jock was in his mid thirties, but we soon found we had a lot in common and came to be very good mates. The ship also carried an asdic technician.

Liverpool, Greenock and Londonderry were the bases of the Atlantic escort groups, and it was to the last named that we steamed a few days later.

This little ship was different in every way from my first ship. There the emphasis had been on speed and gun power, and fighting mainly against aircraft – a different kind of war altogether from what an Atlantic escort vessel would experience.

It seemed so slow and leisurely, after a few days at sea with our first (for me) convoy.

If your mess caterer was a generous-minded kind of a bloke, and liked his food into the bargain, you lived well; but if, on the other hand, he wasn't and didn't, then mealtimes were nothing to get very excited about. There were also, of course, other factors to be taken into account, such as how knowledgeable, enterprising and obliging the cook was. His ability and willingness to control several boiling pots on the top of a bucking stove in an Atlantic gale made all the difference.

There were two messing systems in the Royal Navy. All the larger ships and shore establishments were on the general messing principle. You just accepted for each meal what the navy decided you should have. The meals were adequate, I suppose, but the menus didn't vary overmuch. Smaller ships, such as sloops, corvettes and frigates, employed the canteen messing arrangement. Each mess was allowed a certain amount of money per month to buy from the canteen, and depending on how well or otherwise you ate there would be either a surplus (if your caterer was stingy) or a mess bill to pay (if you lived well).

We took it in turns as 'cooks of the mess', two at a time, for the week. Duties were to keep the mess generally clean and tidy, prepare the meals, dish them up, and wash up afterwards, etc. Some meals were a disaster in the early days, like the time one lad tied his mess joint of meat up with tarred string. Most of us persevered, however, and after a while could make quite reasonable pastries, puddings and fruit cakes.

The term 'big eats' could apply to any good meal, but especially to a supper of eggs, bacon, sausages, chips, tomatoes and baked beans!

Leftovers, or surplus from a meal, was known as 'spares'. Woe betide anyone who called it 'gash' (rubbish). Surplus food only became gash when it was established that no one wanted it. The gash bucket was emptied only at dusk each day. We didn't want to leave a trail of tin cans, cigarette packets, etc. for the U-boats to follow.

A gash chute was a steel tube that led from upper-deck down the ship's side to the waterline. There was one on either side of the ship, and naturally we would always use the one on the lee, or sheltered, side; but it frequently happened that some idiot would use the one on the weather side and get half of it back in his face. Some people never learn.

Crockery and cutlery became very scarce on the mess decks on long-haul convoys, especially if the weather was very bad. Lots of cups and plates would end up in pieces on the deck after either sliding off the table or coming out of the racks, because they had not been secured properly.

Empty condensed-milk tins were retained and became valuable drinking utensils when all the cups had been smashed.

Many items of cutlery disappeared down the gash chute when emptying the washing-up water. One would hear a clatter, and would then stand and solemnly recite a little rhyme:

Tinkle, tinkle, little spoon,
Knife and fork will follow soon.

Mealtimes in bad weather were a bind. It was a continual struggle to keep the food on the plate, and the plate on the table. The table itself did at least stay put, because it was bolted to the deck, although the angle of the top was changing all the time!

The mess stools were not fixed to the deck, and would slide when the ship rolled badly. It was quite a comic situation sometimes, when your stool began sliding away from the table. It required some dexterity and balance to grab your plate before it was out of reach.

"Never heard you ask if you could get down," lads on the other side of the table would say with a grin – themselves tight up against the table. Then it would be their turn as the ship rolled back the other way. We hung our teapot on a piece of twine from the deckhead, where it swung like a pendulum. Actually, of course, the pot stayed still, and the ship rolled round it. We had to keep a wary eye on it in case it cracked us on the head.

Long spells of rough weather were very wearing. The continuous pitching and rolling made everything we did that much more difficult. It was a relief to climb into our hammocks sometimes – that at least neutralised the rolling motion.

Many of the men suffered the miseries of seasickness. How they managed the daily chores and the four hours on watch I will never know! Watchkeeping in exposed positions in the North Atlantic was pretty miserable for anyone, let alone those sufferers. A suggested remedy was frequently heard being offered to those poor devils: a lump of fat pork on a piece of string! How unkind people can be to their friends! I was one of the more fortunate ones. I felt very bad just once, but happily it passed off.

The biggest enemy, apart from the U-boats and the sea itself, was boredom. Tempers became short, and sometimes fists would fly, maybe between men who were the best of friends normally. Really trifling things would be enough to start an argument sometimes. I once saw two chaps almost come to blows over a children's comic paper.

Any kind of reading matter was valuable. I read anything I could lay my hands on, except medical books from the sickbay – I found them depressing.

At one stage I thought I would have a go at writing a book, and I did in fact fill up two or three notebooks. It never did get finished – I decided one night, after reading through it again, that it was absolute rubbish, and threw it away in disgust.

My watch-keeping partner, Jock, was a keen fisherman, and his burning ambition after the war was to build his ideal house. I suppose it is the dream of many men; however, there was a slight difference in Jock's case: the centrepiece and most important part of Jock's house was to be a den to hold his fishing gear! We spent many sessions together, designing houses on scraps of paper.

I became an expert darner of socks, and sometimes mended some for one or two of my messmates. On one occasion I turned and re-taped one of my blue collars – quite a big job this. Getting the three white tapes nice and straight and even was quite a challenge. I don't think I would have the patience, eyesight or nimbleness of fingers to do it now!

I had joined my first ship on the Malta convoys at a critical time, and now also, it seemed, was a critical time in the Battle of the Atlantic. The late summer and autumn of 1942, leading up to the 'black winter', was the worst period of the whole war for merchant-ship losses. New construction was not keeping pace with the sinkings; and although we ordinary mortals didn't know it at the time, it seems we were coming perilously close to losing the battle. Only mass production in American and Canadian yards, when they got really geared up, saved the day.

A new class of freighter, built from prefabricated sections, came into being: the Liberty ship. Many women and young girls were employed in the shipyards, both over there and in the UK, and became expert welders.

There was also a crying need for more escort vessels, as many convoys were sailing with a woeful lack of protection. However, a large number were under construction at this time.

Later on, as they became available, special hunter-killer groups were formed, in addition to the normal convoy-escort groups. At the same time more and more U-boats were coming into service, and they began forming 'wolf packs'. One U-boat would shadow a convoy and direct other U-boats on to it.

Many convoys were severely mauled when subjected to concerted night attacks, and often running battles, lasting several days, were fought with the wolf packs. When the night attacks took place, a prearranged plan was put into operation. At a signal from the escort commander, the escorts nearest the point of attack would fire 'snowflake rockets' to illuminate the area and force the U-boats down, where they could be detected by asdic.

A large convoy would cover several square miles of ocean. The commodore in charge – usually a retired senior naval officer – would be on a leading ship in one of the central columns.

Ships carrying munitions, and tankers, would be placed in the centre of the convoy. All would be expected to keep strictly to their positions. After dark, each ship showed a shaded blue stern light, and towed a drogue – a barrel, perhaps, on a length of rope. Lookouts on the following ship would endeavour to keep this in view, to avoid overrunning. It must have been a nightmare job at night in bad weather, I should think.

Rescue ships, if available, brought up the rear of the convoy. The 'bone collectors', the U-boat crews called them. They called themselves the 'undertakers', their boats the 'hearses'; merchant ships of the convoy were the 'coffins'; and we, the escorts, were dubbed the 'pall-bearers'.

Operating the asdic set at sea was a different kettle of fish from the training-base simulator and the sheltered waters where we had done our training. Out in the Atlantic we found the interference from water noises much more pronounced in our earphones, and when the ship was pitching or rolling heavily in a gale or heavy swell it became very uncomfortable.

The loud ping of the transmission every three seconds, and the crashing and swelling of the water against the dome beneath the ship, coupled with striving to pick out any telltale echo, or diesel hydrophone effect, was very wearing indeed.

We worked in pairs, as I said earlier, and would change over each half-hour as first and second operators. That brought a slight respite – we didn't need to concentrate quite as hard as second operator – but even so, sometimes at the end of the four-hour watch I felt my head didn't belong to me any more. The first sign of becoming 'ping happy', we wondered!

Our first two convoys were quite uneventful, although we did drop two patterns of depth charges on a doubtful contact. Sometimes when off watch in fine weather we would scan the ships of the convoy through a pair of binoculars we had borrowed, and I became quite expert at identifying the silhouettes of different types of ships: the 'flush-decked', the 'three-island', the tankers with the engines aft, the different shapes of the bow and counter, the Liberty ships, the war emergency freighter, and ships with heavy-lift derricks, Samson posts, etc.

Sometimes we recognised old friends we had escorted before, and wondered if we would see them again one day. One of the headaches of every convoy commodore and escort senior officer was the straggler. Often it would be an obviously very old ship, with a tall, skinny funnel. Sometimes we would drop back to try to chivvy it on a bit, and then perhaps it would start making smoke. There would be various reasons for this happening, and not necessarily because they were sloppy or careless, but it could spell trouble for a convoy.

A watchful U-boat several miles away could spot a smudge of smoke on a fine day. U-boats were also equipped with a hydrophone, and could pick up ships' propeller noises at a distance of several miles.

It was too ridiculous for words – the strange sound we were listening to in the middle of the Atlantic in the middle of the night. We both began to wonder if we were having hallucinations. Were we becoming 'ping happy'?

As I remarked earlier, the asdic oscillator was not only a transmitter/receiver but also a hydrophone, or underwater microphone. All kinds of noises were heard, some easily recognised (such as ships' propellers and whooping, whistling and clicking noises from shoals of fish, and individual larger fish), others quite weird and unexplainable, but what we were listening to now beat everything!

Jock was operating the set; I was resting. I had, in fact, just made a mug of cocoa on our little electric stove. This was a bar removed from an electric fire and mounted on a base plate – an essential component of the asdic set, we called it! All kinds of concoctions were heated up during the night watches. A great favourite with ourselves – and the bridge staff when we were feeling a bit generous – was our special stew, or 'pot mess'. Into a container would go various kinds of soups, corned beef, baked beans, tomatoes, etc. As the Chief Yeoman of Signals remarked one night, "I don't know whether I'm supposed to drink it, or eat it with a knife and fork." We occasionally offered the officer of the watch a mugful, which was usually gratefully accepted.

They all also liked our ky (cocoa). 'Pusser's ky' was almost a meal in itself. It came in thick slabs, and we would cut chunks off and melt them down in a saucepan on our stove. Sugar and dollops of condensed milk were added, and it would be so thick sometimes that we could almost stand a spoon up in it.

The term 'pusser', was widely used in the service. Broadly speaking, it meant anything to do with the navy; also smartness, strictness, etc.

Anyway, our refreshments were welcomed by all. Four-hour night watches in exposed positions – especially in bad weather with great waves breaking over the forecastle and icy spray lashing over the bridge – must have been extreme misery. We asdic operators were very lucky to be in our cosy little cabouche, I think.

To get back to the strange noise we were listening to. Both operators wore their earphones at all times, whether actually operating the set or resting. Any unusual hydrophone effect, or echo, would register immediately whether we were reading a book or brewing cocoa.

"What do you think, William?"

I laughed, and replied, "It sounds like a horse galloping down the road, Jock!"

"Just what I thought too," he said.

"Shall we report it, Jock?"

"Aye, we'd better. I expect we'll have some fun now, William. Asdic cabinet bridge," he called through the voice pipe.

"Bridge," came the reply.

"Strange hydrophone effect, green four O," said Jock.

A slight pause, then: "What is strange about it?" asked the officer of the watch.

"Very odd sound," replied Jock. "We've never heard anything like it before."

"Well, what does it sound like?" asked the officer of the watch.

"Like a horse galloping down the road," said Jock.

'I hope you can't hear us laughing,' I thought.

We could hear some muttering through the voice pipe, then a voice asked, "Are you two playing silly buggers?"

"No," said Jock. "Switch your bridge speaker on and see what you think!"

A few seconds elapsed, then: "Officer of the watch speaking. You are dead right. What do you think it is?"

"Probably some kind of fish," replied Jock.

"All right, disregard."

It was quite an amusing incident, and helped to relieve the boredom. Incidentally, the strange noise ceased as abruptly as it had begun.

We sometimes encountered schools of whales, and would get small but quite distinct echoes off them. Another sound which I always associated with whales was a very mournful kind of cry – so very sad, it sounded.

The most distressing noises were heard when ships were going down – grinding and cracking sounds.

Sitting in a comfortable chair in a cosy compartment listening to the myriad sounds from the deep could be quite eerie at times.

The long night watches were boring and often soul-destroying. The continuous pinging noise of the transmissions, and the reverberations, made one's head feel as though it was full of demons dancing around. It was said there was an asylum somewhere ashore where insane submarine detector operators ended their days! I don't know if there was any truth in the story, but sometimes I felt I could nearly believe it.

Long-distance slow convoys were the worst. Sometimes it seemed as though we would never reach our destination – that we would just go on sailing, on and on. Bad weather did nothing to help matters either. Our ship, its designers and constructors came in for some abuse.

Although it was our job, and objective, to detect U-boats, we were not all that anxious to do so – we just hoped they would keep away from our convoy! However, any distraction was welcome sometimes, as witness the 'galloping horse'. We were always pleased when the end of the watch was near.

One other odd incident comes to mind as I write this. Again, it was during one of the long night watches, but it had a happy outcome for one of our operators.

The range recorder held a roll of specially treated paper, and, as it slowly unwound, the transmissions, reverberations and any echoes were recorded on it by a metal stylus. When operating the set, we kept our eyes mainly on the gyro repeater and oscillator indicator, as it stepped round the area we were sweeping. It was an automatic sweep, with the newer 144 and 145 sets, but each time it reached the right-ahead position it had to be manually reset to the starting position, five degrees abaft the starboard and port beams. However, we would glance occasionally at the bearing and range recorders to check that they were functioning correctly, and it was on one such check of the latter that the word 'Derbyshire' appeared, written in pencil. I watched as the paper unwound, and the name of a small town appeared.

I attracted Jock's attention, and he moved round and stood behind me.

Next came a street name and house number, and finally a girl's name.

It may sound trivial, but that small event cheered us up. We were 1,000 miles out in the Atlantic, and getting further from Britain by the minute, but here in front of us was a small but real link with home.

"I wonder what she is like, Jock," I said.

"Write to her, William," he replied. Then he added with a grin, "You might be the very laddie she is looking for."

I didn't, but one of our lads did, and some months later the two met and became very fond of each other. We gathered there was even a prospect of marriage.

I wonder if she thought anything would ever come of it when she stopped her machine in the middle of the night and wrote her name and address.

Anyone who has experienced it will ever remember the stench of fuel oil. It was always present where a ship had gone down. Hateful though the smell was, it didn't cause us any personal injury; but we sometimes came across poor devils in the water who were drenched in oil, coughing and choking.

I had my first experience of it on the Atlantic, on our third convoy, when two ships were sunk one evening. We had just finished our supper when the alarm bells went; then the order over the Tannoy, "Stand by depth charges."

I grabbed my lifebelt and dashed up the nearby ladder to the upper deck. It was fairly dark, although the moon was beginning to rise. As I turned to climb the ladder to the bridge I became aware of a bright glow astern, over our port quarter. I hadn't heard any explosions or gunfire, and I wondered what was going on.

As if in reply to my thoughts, a voice at my elbow said, "Snowflakes going up – two ships hit in the wing column."

My depth-charge action station at this time was on the echo sounder, an instrument that recorded details of any contact we passed over. It was situated in a small compartment to the rear of the wheelhouse, which also happened to be the Captain's sleeping quarters while at sea. I think I must have forgotten about that, because I nearly bowled him over when I went barging in.

"Sorry, sir," I stuttered.

"What is happening?" He shot the question at me as he got into his duffel coat.

"Two ships have been hit in the wing column," I said. "Snowflakes are going up at rear of convoy, sir."

"Which wing, man?" he barked.

"Er – starboard, sir," I replied.

'I don't envy him his job,' I thought as he went clattering up the ladder to the compass platform. 'He has got to take complete control now. He has to make the decisions as escort commander.'

We made a wide 180-degree turn, and went back, but there was nothing to be done. One of the group corvettes had picked up a number of survivors; but, although both of us circled the area for some time, there was no further sign of life.

Both ships had sunk almost immediately. Nothing remained except a few odds and ends of wreckage, and the stench of oil.

A few days later we experienced a much worse smell – one with agonising effects. It is something I will never forget.

It began with a spectacular aerial display. I was off watch at the time – Jock and I had just been relieved at the end of the

119

morning watch (4 a.m. till 8 a.m.). It was a very pleasant morning, already quite warm and the sea almost flat calm – all nice and peaceful.

We decided to stay up top for a bit to get a bit of fresh air, and clear our heads of the four-hours' concentration and the near-5,000 pings! We stood leaning over the side at the after end of the bridge, looking at the columns of ships spread over several square miles of ocean. There were ships of various sizes and types, including several large tankers in the central columns.

"I wouldn't care to be on one of those, William," Jock remarked. "They are brave men," he added.

"They certainly are, Jock," I replied. "I should imagine it is like sitting on the top of a volcano, waiting for it to erupt. When you hear some of the stories from home about petrol being wasted – how some bastard wangled some extra, to go to some race meeting or other, and the spivs and black-marketeers offering anything for a price – it makes your blood boil."

"Aye, William. Scum like that wouldn't lose any sleep worrying about the blokes who are bringing the stuff in. They wouldn't want to know about brave merchant seamen getting blown up – or boiled, roasted or fried! 'Scum' is the right word for them."

We were to see, on a later convoy, what survivors from a burning oil tanker look like, but to get back to where I began:

It was all quiet and peaceful, we thought; then, before our very eyes, the forepart of the fifth ship in the column nearest us erupted in a cloud of smoke and debris. Then we heard the explosion and felt the shock wave.

We stood rooted to the spot as motor-transport tyres flew in all directions – there seemed to be hundreds of them, whirling and spinning through the air and splashing down all around the stricken ship.

She had turned to port out of the column, and appeared to be almost stopped by now, her forepart a mass of flames and smoke.

We turned slightly to starboard to close with her, then watched spellbound as a dense cloud of yellowish smoke poured out of her, close down by the waterline, and began spreading in our direction.

'In a few moments, we will be enveloped by that,' I thought.

"I don't like the look of that, Jock," I said.

Whether someone shouted a warning, or the alarm bells went, I don't remember, but I threw myself down, took as deep a breath as I could, and buried my face in my arms. I held my breath till I felt my lungs were bursting, and then had to gasp for air. Immediately, I felt daggers in my chest, and for about four hours afterwards I was wracked with an agonising cough, but happily I soon recovered.

We learned afterwards that the ship's two forward holds had contained motor-transport tyres and vats of sulphuric acid – earmarked for the Middle East theatre.

When seawater and sulphuric acid mix you get chlorine gas. I hope I never get another whiff of it.

Many merchant ships, with the great mass of their weight low down, settled on a fairly even keel. This gave the crew members who were not in the immediate vicinity of the explosion a reasonable chance to get off. Their worries didn't end there, however. Their chances of being fished out of the water alive were pretty slim sometimes, especially in heavy seas, or on a pitch-dark night.

Warships, with their immense top weight of gun turrets and armour plate, could, when struck by a salvo of torpedoes, roll completely over with a frightening suddenness.

That had happened to the battleship *Barham* during my spell on the Malta convoys. Hit by three torpedoes, she had rolled over on to her side, and then there was a terrible explosion as a magazine blew up. Over half her company were lost.

Every man who went to sea during the war recognised that there was a distinct possibility their ship might be sunk. The thought was always there in our minds, but after a while we didn't let it worry us too much.

My own private fear was of being trapped in a capsized ship, with no chance of getting out.

Men who sailed in ships carrying munitions, or other explosives, had no such worries, I should imagine. There would be a gigantic explosion, then nothing left, apart from a multitude of splashes as wreckage fell back into the water.

Men who sailed in oil or petrol tankers were the real heroes. They knew that if the ship was torpedoed, it could be instantly engulfed in a sea of flames; and even if they were fortunate enough to get off, as likely as not the sea around them would be on fire also.

Refit! The buzz had been going round the ship for days now, and it was finally officially confirmed. There was much speculation as to where it would be. Several characters claimed they knew – places as far apart as Belfast and Chatham Dockyard were mentioned!

Just for fun, and the opportunity of having a little wager, we decided to have a competition. A long list of possible dockyards was compiled, and typed out by one of the ship's writers, and anyone interested backed their fancy at two shillings a time. If no one had backed the correct one, or if it was not on the list, the nearest port to it was declared the winner. This could involve much argument, and measuring up with dividers and ruler! Naturally, we all hoped it would be the nearest port to our hometowns, and when we were told it was to be a small yard on the Humber I was quite satisfied.

On arrival, the starboard watch went off on ten days' leave – port watch to follow when they returned.

It was pretty uncomfortable on board at refit time. Everywhere became a shambles, and our cosy and orderly little world was invaded by all manner of civilians, including welders; steel cutters; electricians; radar, asdic and gunnery technicians; carpenters; painters; and labourers. They seemed to appear from nowhere, and occupied the ship. We wondered if we ought to apologise for getting in their way. They had their job to do, of course, but we were always mighty pleased when they cleared off about teatime.

Asdic and radar ratings shared the same mess on board at

this period, and my shore-going pal was one of the latter. Eric Simpson (Simmo) was from Lincoln. He was quiet, like me. We got on very well together. We both had very pleasant memories of our stay there.

On our first evening ashore, we met up with two very nice girls whilst waiting in the queue for the cinema. Girls seemed attracted to Simmo – I had noticed it before. He wasn't, by any stretch of the imagination, handsome, but there was something about him that attracted them. Anyway, we got into conversation with these two, and after the show we walked them home and were invited in for a cup of tea and to meet their parents, who made us most welcome. That was the beginning of several visits to their homes, where we spent many happy hours playing whist, rummy and dominoes.

We took in a few more cinema shows, and a couple of dances – which I didn't enjoy all that much. I hated the crowded, noisy dance hall – I would much rather have gone for a good walk any time. However, I survived.

On our final meeting, the night before we sailed, we took them several bars of chocolate and some of our cigarettes – just to say thank you. They had been so nice to us.

I enjoyed my ten days at home. 'Up the line' we used to say for going on leave. My parents and young sisters were pleased to see me, and I them, of course. I managed to produce some more chocolate and cigarettes, which were gratefully accepted!

My old workmates on the farm bombarded me with questions – most of which I could not answer.

"I'm just an AB," I said. "Nobody tells me very much."

I could have told them that in this late autumn of 1942 things were not going very well for us in the Atlantic – that lots of our merchant ships were going down, and many brave seamen were losing their lives. I could have told one of them, who was grumbling about the few cigarettes he could get, he was bloody lucky to be getting any at all. I could have told them to get their Home Guard rifles and shoot, out of hand, any selfish and thoughtless people they saw gallivanting around in their cars, wasting precious petrol. I could have told them also – some of them, at least – to be thankful to be sleeping undisturbed in their own cosy beds every night. I don't suppose they would have understood if I had.

There was a rather embarrassing moment on my second night at home. Father invited me to go for a drink at his local, and to meet some of his cronies. I didn't mind doing that in the least, but before we had been there very long the barmaid thought she would like to touch the sailor's collar for luck. Goodness knows what was supposed to be lucky about it, but people would often do that – just a light touch of the hand, and away again. However, the barmaid – a very unnatural-looking blonde – couldn't do it as simply as that. She had to put her arms around my neck and cross them on my shoulders.

'Do you mind!' I thought. 'And you don't have to stand so bloody close either.'

Several of the customers began staring at us, and a party of RAF chaps from the nearby base started making some odd remarks.

One of them started up with "All the nice girls . . ."

'You're more than welcome to this one,' I felt like telling him.

I won't say I thought her repulsive exactly, but I was pleased when she had made her wish and let go.

Father told me of an incident that had occurred a few weeks previously. He had almost reached home (about ten thirty one night, apparently – from his local, I guessed) when he thought he heard a distant sound of twigs snapping, or branches breaking. He didn't think any more about it, but a few days later, when out with his gun, he came to a small wood and noticed the tops of several of the trees were smashed, and bits were scattered about on the ground. About 200 yards further on he came upon a wrecked Mosquito fighter bomber, and lying thirty yards or so out on the field were the bodies of the two crew members. The necks of both of them were broken, and Father said he noticed the watch on the arm of one of them had stopped at about ten thirty.

He informed the local police, and later the same day an RAF

crash-recovery crew arrived and collected the debris. One of them said it was probable that the aeroplane had run out of fuel.

The ten days' leave passed all too quickly, and it was time to catch the train back.

The ship had been a shambles when I left her, and I couldn't see much improvement when I arrived back. Electric cables, air hoses and welding gear were strewn about; empty paint cans and masses of stores were waiting to be sorted out and stowed away, and there was another pile on the dockside.

New and improved radar had been installed, and the operators' cabouche had been fitted on the after end of the bridge, next to our own compartment.

A new anti-submarine weapon had been fitted on the forecastle. Known as a 'hedgehog', it was a multi-barrelled mortar that threw a pattern of twenty-four bombs, with contact fuses, about 300 yards ahead of the ship. It was a great idea, we realised. It would enable the attacking ship to remain in contact right up to the moment of firing. In the conventional depth-charge attack, contact was lost at about that range, when the asdic beam passed over the target. On the other hand, it became clear at once that a hedgehog attack would have to be very accurate, because the bombs would not explode unless they actually hit the target, whereas a depth charge would when its depth setting was reached. A depth charge exploding fifty or sixty feet from a U-boat could cause lethal damage.

There was for and against, we decided.

Two days later, as if by magic, all the dockyard workers and their equipment had gone. Then began the task of clearing up behind them. After considerable sweeping and scrubbing, things began to look more shipshape.

The remaining stores were brought on board, and stowed away, and we were ready for sea. After a last night's leave for the port watch, we sailed the next morning – round the north of Scotland, for Londonderry.

There were cold and dismal faces on the forecastle as we

reeled up the mooring wires, stowed the fenders, and secured for sea.

The morning was cold and dismal too – a light drizzle was falling. Everything looked grey, and we were going back to the war. The forenoon watchkeepers closed up as we left the sheltered waters of the Foyle and headed into the Atlantic rollers. Winter was coming on, and I thought again how fortunate we asdic operators were in our cosy little compartment when I watched the heavily muffled lookouts and gun crews going to their stations.

At least there was some cheerful news: we were going down to a warmer climate, or so the buzz said!

"It's definitely Gibraltar," one of the stokers told me. "Chief got it from one of the subbies."

I hoped he was right.

The general opinion on the mess decks was that we would go anywhere they chose to send us, provided it was not North Russia! I dreaded the thought of Russian convoys. If you got 'ditched up' in those icy waters, your life expectancy was reduced to about one minute.

There had been a scare some weeks earlier when a buzz had gone round the ship to the effect that our next trip would be to Murmansk. When we were ordered up to Loch Ewe a day or two later, it seemed our worst fears had been realised. We knew Loch Ewe was where the convoys to Russia assembled.

We were cheered up a little bit when one of the petty officers stated, "No chance! These little boats aren't suited to the Russian run!"

Petty Officer Harris must know what he is talking about, we thought. He had been in the service about fifteen years. However, on arrival at Loch Ewe, our hopes were dashed again. We had not been at anchor all that long before another buzz went around the mess decks: they were sending a boat out to us with a load of Arctic clothing! To dampen our spirits still further, one chap said somebody he knew had told him he had heard it was already on board.

"I don't bleeding well believe that!" another lad exclaimed. "My oppo is bosun's mate of the other watch, and he would have told me for sure if there had been any boats alongside."

It was buzz and counter-buzz.

Anyway, early the following morning we weighed anchor, left the anchorage, and began escorting two freighters to the south, to join up with a large convoy leaving the Clyde – destination West Africa, and beyond.

That was all past history, however – now we were starting a new journey.

"Definitely Gibraltar," the Stoker had said.

As it turned out, he was partly right: it was a southbound convoy, and some of the ships were destined for Gibraltar. The remainder (and bulk) of them were sailing for Freetown and the Cape.

We didn't actually call in at Gibraltar this time – the local escort force met us, and four of the ships were detached.

The outward journey was quite uneventful up till now, except for a bit of a scare one night when one of the lookouts swore he smelled diesel fumes. There was nothing on the radar, and our asdic set produced no echoes or hydrophone effect. We switched the transmissions off for a minute or two, and listened intently for the sound of diesel engines, but there was nothing.

A few star shells had been fired, but nothing was sighted either. If there had been a U-boat on the surface nearby, emitting diesel fumes, it must have been a phantom one, we decided.

That observation started a discussion on the mess deck – about wraiths and spirits. Had anyone ever seen a ghost, or experienced anything ghostly?

"I reckon I did one day," said a voice.

We all looked at the speaker in anticipation.

"I was an insurance agent before the war, and one afternoon when I called on one of my clients something mighty peculiar happened. As I walked up the drive to the house, I noticed a woman standing in a corner where two walls met. I didn't recognise her as the lady of the house, and wondered idly who she might be. Well, even as I was looking directly at her, she vanished. One second she was there, as plain as you blokes are to me now, and the next she was gone! There was no door or window near where she had been standing, no bushes or anything as simple as that," he concluded.

"I remember my old lady telling me about a queer happening some years ago," remarked one of the others. "Mother had a friend – an elderly spinster lady who used to go and stay at people's houses when they went abroad on holidays and suchlike. Maybe that was how the old dear earned her living – but that don't matter. Anyhow, one particular place she used to go to – a big house, Mother said it was – was supposed to have a ghost, and apparently one time when the owners came back off holiday they said to her, 'I expect you have heard we are supposed to have a ghost.' Then they jokingly asked if she had seen or heard anything? She told them no, but she said she wasn't worried about it anyway. Spirits never hurt anybody, did they? Now, to get to the point of the story," the narrator said: "This old dear was going to bed one night, on a later occasion when she was staying there, when something very strange occurred. She had got almost to the top of the main staircase when she heard voices – the sound of excited young children chuckling and chattering. She climbed the last stair or two and turned to face the landing – quite expecting to see someone, but there was nothing, and the voices faded and were gone."

Pretty creepy, we thought!

"I remember a tale one of the horse keepers on the farm told me," I said. "Three of them were coming to work one winter's morning – they started work half an hour earlier than the rest of us to get their charges into the yard and feed them. It was a frosty morning, and still quite dark. They were walking abreast, this old boy said, when something icy-cold touched his hand.

"'Blast! I drew my arm up something sharp!' he said.

"'Whatever is the matter with you, Ernie?' one of the others asked.

"Well, Ernie told him what had happened, but they couldn't see anything to explain it when they looked around.

"'You must have imagined it, boy,' the others said.

"'I damn well didn't! I don't imagine things,' he told them.

"'Your hand might have brushed against some weeds or grass with a frost on it,' they suggested, but there wasn't any growth more than three or four inches high.

"'That wholly put the wind up me,' the old boy concluded. 'My blood ran right cold.'"

"Any more ghost stories anybody?" someone asked.

"Have any of you lads heard of Borley Rectory – the most haunted house in England?" I asked.

Apparently one or two of the lads had.

"It was between Long Melford and Sudbury on the Essex/ Suffolk border," I said. "The BBC did a broadcast from there one night; it must have been about a couple of years before the war. I remember we sat at home with our ears glued to the old battery portable, but nothing happened at Borley Rectory that night. Anyway, after reading about the ghostly history of the rectory in an article in the local paper at about the same time, my young pal and I thought we would go over on our bikes and investigate! We used to go all over the place on our bikes. Mother would pack us some grub and give us a few coppers to get a bottle of drink somewhere, and we would be out all day sometimes. We planned to hang around the rectory till after dark, and although we both felt pretty scared we did just that. It had said in a newspaper article that a local chap who used to pass the rectory each morning on his way to work had seen the figure of a nun standing by one of the entrance gateposts. He had seen her on a number of occasions, and one morning he stopped and turned to ask if she was all right. She looked so very sad, he said. However, as he took a step or two towards her she just vanished. My young pal and I thought we would check that out. We walked back and forth several times, past the two sets of entrance gates close together, and on the opposite side of the road! We peered anxiously into the shadows hoping and at the same time dreading that a deeper shadow might appear.

Dare we go into the grounds? The ghostly figure of a nun was supposed to flit from the house to a summer house in the garden. No, we didn't think we would go inside! The place had an eerie atmosphere, and I don't think either of us were sorry to leave. We got our bikes and set off on the road for home."

Borley Rectory was mysteriously gutted by fire in 1940. Some modern dwellings now stand on what used to be the garden, but the site of the rectory itself is still derelict – at least it was in 1986, when I was last round that way.

The whaler had been quickly hoisted, swung inboard, and lowered on to its chocks. The roaring and crackling of the flames, the fierce gusts of hot air that hit us and the piteous moaning of one of the survivors was like a ghastly nightmare.

We were shocked at the survivors' appearance when we finally got them on board. Faces and hands were blackened and charred, heads grotesquely swollen. They were barely recognisable as human beings.

"Get them below as quickly as possible," said our ship's doctor, "but be careful how you handle them."

"Chop-chop, lads!" said the buffer, "but gently does it."

There were many willing hands to lift the two men out of the whaler and carry them down to the sickbay, where the tattered remnants of their overalls were removed.

They were lifted gently on to two cot beds while the Doctor prepared to make his examination.

"Right then, lads," said the buffer, "the Doctor needs some elbow room – clear the sickbay. You have done your bit."

It was almost time for the middle watchman to relieve us when we reported an underwater explosion. We switched our main light off, and we heard a rattle on the door as Jim Kirby and Geordie came in to relieve us.

"What's happening?" I asked Geordie as I handed him my headset.

"A tanker has gone up, Matt," he replied, "just as we were coming up the bridge ladder – right in front of our eyes. Bloody great ball of fire rose out of her – awful!"

"Those poor bastards," said Jim, "they didn't stand a chance."
We closed the door behind us and turned to go forward to the ladder. Then Jock and I stopped dead in our tracks.

"God Almighty, William!" said Jock. "Just look at that!"

"Nobody is going to get out of that alive," I said.

There was much activity on the compass platform. Hurried orders were being passed, and the whaler's crew was piped to stand by. Up ahead, we heard the blast of sirens as other ships in line astern of the tanker made emergency turns to avoid her, and all around – for miles around, it seemed – was the glow from that awful fire.

The ship itself was a raging inferno, and a wide river of fire was spreading out over the water on one side of her.

I suddenly realised our engines were stopped, and we were gradually closing the gap between us.

"What the hell are we hanging about for?" a voice exclaimed. "There ain't going to be any survivors from that. We'll just be a bloody sitting duck ourselves if that U-boat is still hanging around."

Probably everybody on the upper deck shared his views, but we were all wrong. Somebody's sharp eyes had picked out two dots bobbing in the water.

The whaler's davits had been turned out, and the boat was lowered to deck level. The crew jumped in, and she was quickly lowered and 'slipped'.

There was another explosion from the tanker, and blazing fuel spewed out on the near side. The heat was becoming unbearable, even at the distance we were lying. Flames were creeping over the water between us, but the whaler had reached the swimmers, and a couple of spare hands had struggled to get the men over the side and on to the boat.

A cheer had gone up when she reached the ship's side, just below us. The falls were quickly attached, and the ship began to gather way almost before the whaler had left the water.

A small party of lads gathered in the sickbay the following morning, enquiring after the survivors. We were shocked at their appearance. The Doctor and sickbay attendant were dressing the burns on one of the men's hands.

Noticing our anxious looks, I suppose, the Doctor nodded his head in the direction of the men's faces and said, "Looks worse than it is. Outer layers of skin charred by intense heat – we will begin stripping it off in a few days, as it becomes detached. I don't think there will be any lasting damage there. I am more concerned with the burns on the back of their thighs, and this one's hand."

His hand looked awful. The burns were probably caused by red-hot guard rails, when he scrambled to get off the ship, someone suggested.

A small hose was attached to the ventilation shaft overhead, and some of us would go in when off watch and direct cool, soothing air over the burned areas.

Just as the Doctor had said, the burned skin began flaking off after a few days and patches of new pink baby skin began to appear.

Both men were making good progress when we landed them a week or so later. One of them, in fact, had become quite chirpy.

It was just two days since the Gibraltar-bound ships had left us. Not a bad little number, we thought, the Gibraltar local escort force – plenty of shore leave. They didn't put the sea time in that we did, and there were certainly no long-haul ocean convoys for them.

On the second night, a radar contact was obtained by the corvette on the rear starboard flank of the convoy, and we turned back to assist in a sweep of the area. Star shells, fired by the corvette, illuminated the scene, and one of the bridge lookouts reported seeing a conning tower, but it disappeared almost immediately as the U-boat dived.

We swept a 30-degree sector, covering that bearing, and shortly obtained an echo. It was not very clear, and difficult to hold in the disturbed water in the wake of the convoy. It was lost altogether shortly afterwards. It appeared our corvette companion was having better luck, as she made an attack and dropped a pattern of charges.

A patch of oil was reported, but that in itself was not proof of a kill.

We carried out another sweep of the area, but no further contact was obtained, and it was decided to call off the search.

The dull rumble of an explosion was heard shortly after, and distress rockets went up over on the other side of the convoy.

It seemed there were two U-boats snapping at our heels.

We dropped a pattern of charges on a doubtful contact, with no visible result, as we began to catch up with the convoy.

We had almost caught up with the rear ships when the tanker was torpedoed. It was an unhappy night, but swift retribution was to follow.

"Echo bearing."

'Ping-ing-ing-ing-ing. Pink! Ping-ing-ing-ing-ing. Pink!'

It was exactly seven o'clock in the morning watch and we heard it, sharp and clear – there could be no mistaking what it was.

Jock sat bolt upright in his chair, and settled his earphones more firmly in place. I glanced round at him, and he nodded his head vigorously.

I turned my head back to the voice pipe to report, "Asdic cabinet bridge."

"Bridge," came the reply.

"Echo bearing: green one O. Range: 2,400."

Initial reports were always given as relative bearings – that is, relative to the ship's head. Thus green ten degrees would always be just off the starboard bow – red ten degrees would refer to a similar position off the port bow, and so on down either side to right astern. This method gave the officer of the watch and lookouts an immediate idea of the general direction of the contact or sighting, as the case might be, irrespective of what course the ship was actually steering.

All our subsequent reports would then be given as compass bearings.

'Ping-ing-ing-ing-ing. Pink! Ping-ing-ing-ing-ing. Pink!'

"Asdic cabinet bridge."

"Bridge."

"Bearing: one one O. Range: 2,200 yards."

"Bridge – asdic cabinet. Classify."

'Ping-ing-ing-ing-ing. Pink! Ping-ing-ing-ing-ing. Pink!'

It was a perfect echo, slightly high in pitch. The submarine (there was no doubt in my mind now) was coming at a slight angle towards us, and moving down the starboard side.

'Ping-ing-ing-ing-ing. Pink! Ping-ing-ing-ing-ing. Pink!'

A quick glance at the range recorder – 2,000 yards.

"Asdic cabinet bridge."

"Bridge."

"Left cut on, one two O degrees. Right cut on, one two four degrees. Centre bearing: one two two. Range: 1,900 yards. Echo slight high – bearing moving starboard. Submarine!"

The alarm bells went almost immediately, and 'standby depth charges' was piped.

We could hear through our bridge voice pipe hurried orders being passed. Through our slightly open door came the sounds of boots clattering on iron ladders, and on the deck below, as the gun crews closed up.

Down in the stern of the ship, the depth-charge crews would be waiting for the order to put the depth settings on the charges. They were detonated by a hydrostatic pistol in the primer. Patterns consisted of either five or ten charges. The first, centre and last charges of the patterns rolled off the rails at the stern of the ship. Other charges were hurled out simultaneously to either side, propelled by explosive charges on the throwers.

"Bridge asdic cabinet – attacking!"

There were three operators on the set now, striving to hold on to that elusive echo.

'Ping-ing-ing-ing. Pink! Ping-ing-ing-ing. Pink!'

Doppler (echo pitch) was changing.

"Asdic cabinet bridge."

"Bridge."

"Echo moderate high. Range: 1,500 yards. Bearing steadying. Centre bearing: one three O degrees."

'Ping-ing-ing-ing. Pink! Ping-ing-ing-ing. Pink!'

"Echo marked high. Range: 1,200 yards. Bearing moving port!

Centre bearing: one two six degrees. He's turning again; he's coming right round. Bearing moving port. Centre bearing: one two O degrees. Range: 750 yards."

The ship's head began to swing as port helm was applied. Our object was to pass just ahead of the target and hope he ran into the pattern of charges, but of course he would take evasive measures also.

A violent change of course in the final stages of the attack could make all the difference between a hit or a miss. Charges needed to explode within fifty feet or so of a U-boat to cause lethal damage, although of course charges exploding at a greater distance could smash delicate instruments, smash light bulbs, cause minor leaks in the hull, and also, I should imagine, play havoc with the occupants' nerves.

An avoiding tactic employed by U-boats was the 'bubble target', or asdic decoy. A chemical was released into the water, and it would form bubbles. The echoes obtained from these would not fool an experienced asdic operator, but they could cause enough interference for the U-boat to twist and turn away behind its screen of bubbles.

Another ruse was to release some oil or minor debris from one of the torpedo tubes – pieces of wood panelling, items of clothing, etc. I don't think this was ever regarded as certain confirmation of a kill, however.

'Ping-ing-ing. Pink! Ping-ing-ing. Pink!'

"Asdic cabinet bridge. Bearing moving port – echo the same. Range: 600 yards."

Our ship's head swung further to port. The Doppler was changing again.

"Echo moderate to low. Bearing steadying. Centre bearing: one one two degrees. Range: 500 yards."

'Ping-ing. Pink! Ping-ing. Pink!'

The transmission rate increased as the range shortened.

"Echo marked low. Bearing steady. He is going directly away from us now. Bearing moving starboard. Range: 350 yards. He has turned a complete circle – too late for us to come round again. We are going to pass astern of him!"

'Ping. Pink! Ping. Pink!'

"Instantaneous echoes. Stand by charges. First and throwers, *fire!*" A slight pause, then: "Centre charge, *fire!* Last charge, *fire!*"

There was not much chance of a kill – he must have been well clear of our pattern – but the most important thing now for the operators was to slide the earphones forward. The terrific crash of those explosions could cause permanent damage to the ears.

All eyes on the upper deck were searching astern of us now as the exploding charges sent great spouts of water up.

Back to business again now as the asdic operators tried to regain contact astern: but this was always most difficult, owing to the disturbance the explosions had caused.

We swept and re-swept a designated sector several times, but without result.

"Asdic cabinet bridge – lost contact."

Meanwhile, one of the corvettes of our group had joined in the hunt, we learned, and shortly made her run in on a contact.

We turned on to the bearing, and began sweeping a 30-degree area ahead of us. Shortly after this we reported a rumble of explosions – a pattern of depth charges, we thought – and almost immediately we began to obtain echoes on the same bearing, from the disturbed water caused by the explosions.

We regained contact with the U-boat shortly after, and made a second attack, as did the corvette, but without visible result. After twenty minutes of further patient searching we were in contact again and made our third attack.

The bows and forepart of the U-boat rose vertically out of the water astern of us, amidst towering columns of water thrown up by the depth charges. A boat – forty feet of it, black and sinister – appeared to hover for a few seconds, then flopped down. Was this the swine that had sunk two of our ships? Whether it was or not, one thing was for sure: this one was not going to sink any more ships!

Almost immediately, our after three-inch gun began firing, as did the Oerlikons that would bear. Our corvette companion was also firing – we could see puffs of smoke from her forward gun.

The U-boat was completely surfaced now, and appeared to be on an even keel. Some of her crew were attempting to get their guns working, while others could be seen jumping into the water.

Our two ships were circling the target, and gradually closing in. I don't know if any of our shells scored hits; but, judging by the splashes, there were some mighty near misses.

Snatches of conversation began coming through the bridge voice pipe: "Enough time wasted – we must catch up with the convoy. Ram it!"

"Prepare to ram," was piped. "Forward gun crew, secure and fall out."

"Bridge asdic cabinet – switch the set off."

The ship began to shudder as the speed was increased. We were doing every last little bit of our not all that many knots, I thought, as I held on to a stanchion and kept my eyes glued ahead.

A few more members of the U-boat's crew could be seen jumping into the sea as we got closer and closer.

There was a tremendous crash and grinding of metal as we hit it just forward of the conning tower. Our ship staggered and the bows rose up and over. The water swirled and foamed, and it was all over.

The petty officer of the watch was shouting in my ear: "We shall get a nice bit of leave after this lot. Our bows – be a dry-dock job for sure!"

Several heads could be seen bobbing about as we swung round. Scrambling nets were thrown over the side, and as we came to a stop the swimmers were helped on board.

"Chop-chop!" the buffer was shouting. "We don't want to be hanging around here too long – he may have a friend with him!"

One man had a broken leg, and a section of the guard rail was lowered to help get him on board. There were fifteen of them altogether. They were the few lucky ones. Probably twice as many had gone to their deaths, trapped inside the U-boat. Some of them looked little more than boys. Most were quite calm and collected in spite of their ordeal.

The last one to come up was a fanatical party member, it seemed. He came stiffly to attention and raised his right hand in the Nazi salute.

"Heil Hitler!"

"Heil Hitler, my arse," shouted the buffer.

He placed a foot in the German's middle, gave a mighty shove, and he was back over the side and in the water.

"Now come back up and salute properly," the buffer shouted.

He was placed in the cells, and was closely watched at all times. First thing every morning, apparently, and last thing at night, he came to attention, and *'heiled'* Hitler!

All were taken down to the bathroom and given dry clothes. In a sense, they were not the enemy any more; they were fellow seamen in distress, like many of our own seamen we had picked up.

Watching some of them standing in front of a mirror, carefully combing their hair, it was hardly possible to believe they had just been through about two hours of hell. Fifty depth charges had been dropped on them, and then they had been blown to the surface and bombarded by our guns. There was no doubt about it: they were brave men, those U-boat crews – all volunteers, I believe.

Our captain, a three-ring commander, gave us a talk about it later. He had served in submarines apparently in the First World War, and he described what conditions must have been like in the U-boat when it came up end on.

"Indescribably terrible," he said. "Men would have been thrown down in heaps, crushed by heavy machinery breaking loose, burnt by acid escaping from the batteries. We all know from our own recent experience", he concluded, "what sulphuric-acid burns look like."

Asdic and radar operators shared the same mess. There were roughly the same number of us as there were U-boat survivors, so possibly it seemed a good idea to somebody to move us out and put them in our place. They were, of course, under the watchful eyes of armed guards at all times. They seemed to like our food, coffee and cigarettes. Most of them looked quite happy and relaxed; one or two were morose and sullen.

"Keep an eye on those bastards," the crusher warned the guards. "We don't want them getting up to any mischief." (The crusher was the ship's policeman – regulating petty officer.)

We managed to get a bit of conversation going, and gradually learned that they really believed the war was nearly won – Britain was on her knees!

Their spokesman, with his smattering of English and sign language, indicated this: "England kaput. Englander ships all go." He held out his fist, with the thumb pointing downwards.

Naturally there were some unprintable replies from us.

"Germany kaput – Hitler kaput. Whoever wins the war," said one lad, "one thing is for sure: you bastards have lost!"

I think their illusions were shattered the following morning, when they were brought up on deck for exercise.

We were escorting a very large convoy on this occasion, and our captain had manoeuvred the ship into the centre of it.

"Bring those prisoners up," he ordered.

When they looked around and saw ships everywhere, their faces fell, and I should imagine their spirits fell also. It was pretty obvious they had been fed all manner of lies to keep their morale up.

We had them on board for about two weeks, and, to give them credit, we found on returning to our mess that it was the cleanest and most orderly we had ever seen it. The chaps that had been guarding them told us they had scrubbed and polished everything each morning. One of them had slightly blotted their copybook apparently. He was about to throw some rubbish through the open porthole – strictly forbidden in daylight hours.

We became quite friendly generally, and, odd as it may seem, two or three of them indicated they would like to stay with us!

On arrival at our destination, they were blindfolded and taken ashore. They would, we were informed, probably be going to a POW camp in Canada.

At about this time we thought we had seen the last of 'Mac' – James McKinnon, to give him his full name. A chartered accountant in civilian life, he was a very intelligent and forceful character – a born leader, we all thought. Apparently some of those higher up thought so also, and he was recommended for a commission. Anyway, he became a CW candidate (Commissions and Warrants), one of those in-between characters, we called them – 'not one of us any more, nor yet one of them'.

"Why do you want to go and leave us?" asked one of his messmates. "We had just about decided you were a reasonable human being, and not too bad to live with – now you want to move in with those pigs down aft. Ain't we good enough any more?"

Mac gave a little grin and replied, "It's not certain I'm going yet. I have to go before a selection board – they may not think me suitable material."

"Anyway," he added, "It was not my idea. I have been quite happy here with you lot – miserable bastards that you are!"

Mac left us when we arrived back at our home port, and I for one was convinced it was the last we would see of him.

Most of the ship's company went on a welcome spell of leave while temporary repairs were carried out on our damaged bows.

It was a long, tiring journey home from Northern Ireland, first by train to Larne, where we boarded the ferry to Stranraer; then the long journey down to Euston, sometimes standing or sitting in the corridor; then across London to Liverpool Street; and by train to Cambridge, where there might be a connection for Newmarket if I was lucky.

The journey began with an amusing incident – or a disgusting one, depending on your viewpoint.

Several of the lads visited the nearby bars while waiting for the train at Londonderry Station, and one in particular, a three-badge able seaman by the name of Jack Martin (variously known as Stripey, Jacko or Marty), who should have known better, got well and truly drunk. We all suspected that drink was probably the reason he was, after many years service, still an able seaman – but that was Stripey's business. He was half carried on to the train by some of his mates, and we were to find out a short while later that he had brought a bottle of rum with him. We were only a few minutes out of the station when we heard a crash and commotion in the corridor just beyond our compartment. One of the lads got up and looked out to see what it was all about, then turned to us and said, "Have a butcher's at this, you lot!"

We crowded round him, and there, on his hands and knees, was Stripey, lapping up rum off the floor, which was none too clean. He had cut his mouth and hands on broken glass – he looked terrible.

"God Almighty!" exclaimed one lad. "What a bloody state to get in!"

'What a way to start your leave!' I thought.

Speaking of going on leave reminds me of the ordeal it could be getting across London during the war, sometimes in the middle of an air raid. I will always remember the obstacle course the Underground stations became – stepping over people on the platforms, on the stairways, etc. Whole families and their friends and neighbours had their regular sleeping places. There were bodies everywhere. Happy-go-lucky, they had a great spirit, the Londoners, and they could take anything in their stride, it seemed.

I travelled down on one leave with a London lad – he was from Bermondsey. As the train neared London, I told him of the trouble I had sometimes on the last stage of the journey.

"I can get to Cambridge all right, Terry," I said, "but often that seems to be the end of the line."

"What do you do then?" he asked.

"Hitch a lift if I can," I replied. "Once I walked most of the way. It's about twelve miles from Cambridge Station to my home. I think my best bet is to get a train for Ipswich on the Colchester line later this afternoon. I can get a connection there for Ely and Peterborough – that train stops at a little station just the other side of Newmarket, where the local mail van meets it. I can get a lift into Newmarket on that. I have gone that way before, Terry. It takes a bit longer, that's all."

"It's murder getting about, Matt," he replied, "with the delays and diversions and never enough room on the train. I came all the way down from Glasgow once squatting in the bloody corridor. I kept trying to doze off, but every few minutes somebody was blundering into my legs on their way to the toilet. I just had a thought, Matt – you're welcome to come home with me if you want to kill an hour or two. We can go down to my boozer, if it ain't been blown up, get a few pints down us and have a little bit of fun maybe."

I thanked him and said, "I appreciate it, Terry, but I think I will get over to Liverpool Street, freshen up a bit and get something to eat."

"Suit yourself, Matt. You're welcome any time you want to come – stay the night any time if you're stranded," he added.

"I'm sure I am, Terry," I said, "but I think I will push on. Thanks all the same."

Terry meant well, but I was none too keen on his idea of a little bit of fun. I think it meant getting into a fight, if possible – or a bundle, as he called it. He was a bit of a bruiser, and was always ready and willing to take on anybody without too much excuse or provocation.

I remember hearing him tell his messmates, after a long weekend leave sometime earlier, "Had a great time Saturday night – had about eight pints of wallop, and a bundle with a pongo in the boozer." When asked by one of his mates what had started it, he had replied, "Don't know – nothing really – I think we just thought we would have a go at each other!"

A sad incident occurred in London on a previous spell of leave. Actually I was returning from leave at the time. Having an hour or two to spare before my train left for Scotland, I decided to get a snack at a canteen not too far from Euston Station. I hadn't gone far when my attention was attracted to a figure a little distance ahead of me – a woman's figure. She was moving quite slowly – walking with some difficulty, it seemed – and as I began to catch up with her she appeared to sway once or twice.

'Is she drunk?' I wondered.

Somehow I didn't think so. When I had almost caught up

142

with her, she stopped, swayed again, and seemed about to fall in front of me.

I took hold of her arm to support her, turned to face her, and asked, "Are you all right?"

She was in her late twenties, I guessed. Her face was white and drawn – she looked awful.

"My legs," she muttered, "my legs!"

"What is the matter?" I asked.

"Glass in my legs."

I glanced down, and was shocked to see they were wrapped in bandages, bloodstained in places, right down to her ankles. She swayed again, and I took hold of her other arm. I thought she was going to collapse any second.

"You shouldn't be wandering about like this," I said. "You should be in hospital."

"I came out," she replied. "Lots of people there."

"What happened to you?" I asked.

"My flat – the bombs. Got glass in my legs."

"What are you going to do?" I asked. "Where are you going?"

"I don't know," she whispered.

'What am I going to do with you?' I thought. 'I have a train I must catch pretty soon.'

"Have you any family here?"

"No," she replied, "at Nottingham."

"If I were going home on leave, instead of going back to my ship, I would take you with me," I said. "You could stay with my family for a while – they would look after you. But I must get back to my ship. Perhaps we can find a first-aid post or something."

I was getting rather concerned by now, for my own sake as well as hers. If I missed my ship, I would be in real trouble. Salvation came in the unlikely form of the air-raid sirens.

'Hell!' I thought. 'That's all we need.'

Suddenly a voice, shouting from a little distance along the street, came to the rescue: "Hi, you too, get under cover. Do you want to get your bloody heads blown off! Over here – come on."

I helped her across the road to the shelter, and said to someone who seemed to have some authority, "She has been hurt. Can you help?"

"OK, Jack," was the reply. "We'll see she is all right."

"I will have to go," I said, "or I will miss my train."

Bombs were falling, and the glow of several fires lit the sky as I sprinted for the station. I was only just in time – the train was about to pull out.

I often wondered what happened to her – poor girl.

Our shipmate James McKinnon rejoined us on the morning we sailed, after completing our repairs. Several of us crowded around, plying him with questions.

He held one hand up and said, "In a nutshell, they didn't want me."

We couldn't believe our ears.

"What do you mean, Mac? Why not?"

"I didn't fit their requirements. To be more accurate," he added, "my background didn't."

"What's that supposed to mean?" someone asked.

"Well," he replied, "they asked all sorts of questions about my family, and the kinds of things I did, and one stuffed shirt wanted to know what pack I hunted with. When I replied that I didn't hunt, they lost interest."

"Hunt!" exclaimed Ted Stevens. "What the hell were they on about? What has hunting got to do with fighting a bloody war?"

"Didn't you know, Ted?" a voice asked. "Haven't you heard? They are going to do away with you ping operators, and hunt the U-boats with packs of bloody dogs!"

Another voice broke in: "Yeah, that's right, Ted, fit them all out with water wings – tally bloody ho!"

There followed a chorus of baying and yapping dogs.

"The hunting crowd wouldn't like you calling them dogs," I remarked.

"What do you mean, Matt?" asked Ted.

"They call them hounds," I replied.

"They are still dogs," remarked someone. "They ain't

bleeding cats or canaries. You know what it's all about, though – don't you? – Mac ain't got the right kind of voice."

"I think I speak good English," Mac said with a grin. "Better than some of you bastards! Those Geordies and Scousers – I can't understand a bloody word they say!"

"That's not the point, Mac," came the reply. "You haven't got a plummy voice." The speaker looked around at us all and said, "Don't you poor sods know, if you haven't got a plummy voice, you're not wanted in the bleeding wardroom."

"What was the actual reason they gave for turning you down, Mac?" I asked.

"As far as I can make out," he replied, "unsuitable background."

'What a waste!' I thought, but I believe Mac was secretly pleased to be back with us.

"Gibraltar," the buzz said!

There seemed to be general agreement regarding our destination this trip, and it proved correct. We didn't mind this run too much – it wasn't all that far from home, and we usually managed several runs ashore before we made the return journey.

We often wondered how many German agents were watching our movements from across the bay, in neutral Spain, noting the departure times of our convoys and the movement of warships attached to the base.

As I remarked earlier, the long, slow ocean convoys were for the most part boring and soul-destroying, but we did have a break when the invasion of North Africa took place. We were one small escort vessel in a huge armada of ships that passed through the Straits of Gibraltar heading for French Algeria. Ships of all sizes and types, from huge, menacing battleships to little sloops, corvettes and trawlers, and from great passenger liners, carrying troops of the invasion force, to ammunition ships and freighters, were carrying their vehicles and equipment and supplies. With us were headquarters' ships, depot ships and assorted troop- and vehicle-landing craft.

Once the armies had become established ashore, we spent a month or so in the area, engaged on local escort duties between Oran, Algiers, and Casablanca. I thought Algiers and Casablanca were quite fascinating. Whilst everything back in the UK was drab and grey, total blackout, with little or nothing in the shops and everything in short supply, here was a land of plenty, completely untouched by the war, it seemed. Streets and buildings were brilliantly lit; large stores were crammed full of goods of every description – and most of the things were unobtainable back home. I remember in particular one large store that had counter after counter of cosmetics (lipsticks by the thousand, it seemed) and endless bottles of perfume and all the other things girls liked to put on themselves. Everyone bought as much as they could afford to take home. I believe we were allowed up to half a pint of perfumes duty-free. I also bought some lengths of dress material for my sisters. Algiers was like a fairyland.

During the autumn and winter of 1942/3 U-boats had taken a terrible toll on our shipping; but by the spring the tide had begun to turn, and in the month of May alone a staggering total of forty-one U-boats were sunk.

New weapons and radar, more escort vessels and, most important of all, vastly increased long-range air patrols had tipped the balance in our favour. The Atlantic air gap – the 'black pit', previously beyond the range of shore-based aircraft – had been closed. The Battle of the Atlantic, if not yet over, was being won.

It was in the month of May 1943 also that the Axis forces in North Africa surrendered. Soon they would be cleared out of the Mediterranean theatre altogether. No more Malta convoys from either direction! The sea lanes right through to the Suez Canal would be free and safe for our shipping once again. However, it was not nearly over yet.

In the Atlantic, convoys of merchant ships were still sailing with their escort vessels spread around them. Asdics were still pinging away, searching beneath the surface. Lookouts were still scanning the immediate vicinity through their binoculars, for a conning tower, the tip of a periscope or its wash, or the telltale wake of a torpedo. Radar was still searching further afield. Ships were still being sunk, and men being killed, but on nothing like the same scale as before.

By the end of the war, the Allies were to have lost over 2,500 merchant ships, but the U-boats paid a high price also. Over 750 were destroyed; and of the 40,000 or so men who sailed in them, nearly 30,000 lost their lives.

By the summer of 1943, a U-boat was lucky if it survived more than two or three patrols. At this time, their losses were becoming so severe in the vital areas that they were forced to withdraw to less dangerous waters.

Towards the end of 1943, the first boats with the *Schnorchel* breathing apparatus came into service. This enabled a U-boat to charge its batteries whilst lying submerged, so it was in less danger of being spotted by an aircraft, or detected by radar.

Apparently, the apparatus had only limited success, as waves would often wash over the exhaust flap, close it and fill the boat with diesel fumes.

The homing torpedo was also introduced into the battle about this time. It homed in on a ship's propeller noise, but it was quickly countered by a noise-making device towed some distance astern of the ship.

A new anti-submarine weapon made its appearance about this time also. It was known as a Squid – a three-barrel mortar, which threw its 100-pound projectiles ahead of the attacking ship.

Life for the men on the escorts went on much the same as before: days and weeks of frustration and boredom. It seemed worse now, we agreed. Was it because we were heartily sick of the war, or because most of the danger and excitement had gone?

What would it be like after the war was over? we wondered. Would we be able to settle down to a humdrum eight-to-five job again?

One thing we were all convinced of: it was going to seem different.

We went back to Casablanca and Algiers for a month or so. While at Algiers, a party of five of us had to polish up on our oarsmanship for the Captain's whaler's crew. I'm not sure if this was because our little motor skimmer had broken down, or because our old captain decided he would be different and show off a bit. Anyway, the whaler's crew was piped to fall in one morning.

"You lads are being highly honoured," the buffer told us. "Our captain has decided to do his visiting in the whaler. Now, I'm sure you wouldn't want to let him down and show how bleeding slovenly you are, would you?"

One of our small party mumbled a reply of some sort.

"Well then, lads, you'd better get in that boat and get some practice in. Chop-chop!"

We had several sessions in the next day or two. Our coxswain was one of the seaman petty officers. He seemed worried stiff at the prospect.

"For Christ's sake, don't let me down," he said, "when we've got the old boy on board."

We swaggered around the ship in between sessions – no mess or part-of-ship duties for us, thank you – we in our best uniforms! The Captain's whaler's crew we were.

"Big-headed, creeping bastards!" one of our mates called us.

We rowed the old boy around several times while we were there, taking him on visits to other ships, and to the jetty when he wanted to go ashore. He sat there with a smug look on his face, returning salutes to other ships when we passed close by them. I thought our coxswain looked a bit smug too. Well he might – we were a good crew. We thought we were, anyway. Oars dipped exactly together, with hardly a ripple – a long hard pull, and out of the water cleanly.

The Captain didn't say anything, so, as our coxswain told us afterwards, we "couldn't have looked too bad"!

We escorted one or two more convoys without incident, and then it was D-Day and we gathered with a great mass of shipping in the English Channel. Some troops were already ashore; others were in the process of landing; thousands more were following up. Battleships, lying well off the coast, were firing their great guns at German positions. Monster fifteen-inch and sixteen-inch shells were roaring overhead like express trains. There was no sign of the Luftwaffe – they had been driven from the skies – although an 'odd' aircraft was sighted by one of the lookouts the following evening as the light was fading.

When asked what was odd about it, he replied, "It hasn't got any engines, but it has a light in its tail!"

I think the bridge thought he had gone batty, but we learned later that it was one of the first doodlebugs.

Disaster almost befell us the following morning, although it was quite serious enough anyway. I was making my way below after the completion of the morning watch at the time. It was very foggy – the bridge staff had seemed rather anxious, I thought. I had just reached the bottom of the ladder, and turned to go to my mess, when through the open porthole directly in front of me I saw the sharp bows of a ship emerge from the fog. I shouted a warning to some of my messmates who were sitting and lying around on the stools. The alarm bells rang in the same instant as I grabbed hold of the side of the ladder and braced myself for the crash.

There was a grinding and screeching of tearing metal and the ship lurched sideways. If I had not hung on tightly, I would have been thrown to the deck for sure. I reached instinctively for my lifebelt, then realised I was not wearing it. I should have been, but I had been a bit careless and left it hanging on the bulkhead in the mess.

A chaotic sight met me when I turned to go forward. The bows of a corvette were embedded in our side, almost up to the centre line. There was more screeching of metal as she began to go slowly astern. Steam was roaring from a fractured pipe, the electric circuits were sparking and sputtering, and oil was spurting up from a ruptured tank.

As the other ship drew clear, we began to get some idea of

the damage. There was a gaping hole in the side, about fifteen feet in length, the same at our feet, and daylight streaming in from above, for the bulkhead at the forward end of my mess had been mangled up with the side plates, which had been split open and curled round inwards.

The ship began to list uncomfortably to port, and I imagine the thought was in everyone's mind: 'We have got to get the hell out of this, and on to the upper deck – just in case.'

As I paused to tie my lifebelt tape securely, there was a muffled cry from somewhere in the wreckage.

I shouted to some of the lads who were on their way up the ladder, and to others waiting their turn at the bottom, "There is somebody trapped in that lot!"

Members of the damage-control party arrived at the same time, and it was soon established just where the trapped man was. Tackles and winches were set up, and the mass of twisted steel was hauled sufficiently apart to release him. He had suffered a broken leg and a nasty head injury, but happily we were only a few hours' steaming from Plymouth and he was soon in hospital there. We shuddered to think what might have happened to him. We learned afterwards that he had been asleep on one of the stalls in the next mess.

About twenty-five of us from the two messes affected were lodged in Devonport Barracks while temporary repairs were carried out.

We were soon at sea again when they had been completed, on local convoy duties in the English Channel.

We met a few of the recently liberated French when we put into a small fishing harbour for a few days. They made a great fuss of us – it was almost embarrassing! We were offered huge quantities of fresh fish, onions and other vegetables.

My shore-going pal and I took one family who had made us very welcome a couple of tins of tobacco and a few handfuls of coffee on our second visit, also a few bars of chocolate for their children. They were overjoyed, especially with the coffee.

After another week or two messing about in the Channel, we

were back on the Gibraltar run. The outward journey was quite uneventful, but on the return trip a terrible storm blew up. Soon the ocean was like a wild mountainous landscape. We rolled over and back again almost on to our beam ends. Everything around us creaked and groaned, and we cast countless anxious glances at our patched-up side. Would the repair hold? we wondered. Three long girders had been fitted across the damaged section, and side plates welded to them, but what worried us most was that the two transverse bulkheads that had been buckled and broken had not been replaced. Put another way, there was a long side section with no right-angled support.

The wind blew stronger on the second day, and the sea rose even higher. It did nothing for our morale when the shipwrights arrived and began shoring up the damaged section with huge baulks of timber, and even less when one of them was heard to remark, "If we get an engine failure, or lose the bleeding rudder, we're goners!"

"Miserable bastard!" muttered Geordie.

"It's a fact," replied the shipwright. "We've got to keep heading into it – if we get turned broadside on, we've had it."

Lifelines had been rigged on the upper deck, and it was piped over the Tannoy that no one was to go up top unless it was essential. We learned that a huge sea had broken over the port whaler and smashed it to matchwood, while down below the mess decks were a shambles – water was sloshing backwards and forwards with the movement of the ship, and gear of various kinds was floating about in it. Most of the crockery was in pieces on the deck, and everything that could possibly come adrift seemed to have done so. It became almost impossible to walk from one point to another without holding on to something, in spite of our well-tried sea legs.

We kept an asdic watch throughout the five days of storm, but it was a complete waste of time really. The crashing and banging in our earphones, as the ship plunged down into the troughs, would have drowned out any echoes there might have been, and it was very doubtful if any U-boats that might have be around would have been up anywhere near the surface.

Conditions became so bad on the third day that the convoy was ordered to disperse – each ship to proceed independently. From that morning on, we and one solitary merchantman kept station on each other. Whether it was by design, or otherwise, I don't know. At times she was several cables' lengths away, and at others we seemed to be in imminent danger of colliding with each other.

After coming off watch at midday, I stood on the bridge, holding on to a stanchion, and watched for ten or fifteen minutes. Spray was coming right over the bridge, and the wind howled and shrieked through the stays and signal halyards. The deck was pushed up hard under my feet as the ship rose on a huge wave, then it fell away drunkenly and I felt as though I was floating in the air as we crashed down into a trough. The bows disappeared and a great mass of water boiled and foamed over the forecastle, and a cloud of spray lashed over the bridge.

Our merchantman companion was making heavy going of it also, I noticed. Her stern reared up at a crazy angle, rudder and screw clear of the water. One minute I was gazing down on to her upper deck; the next the positions were reversed, and she appeared to be balanced precariously on a cliff top above us. There would be a slight lull as the sea flattened out a bit, and we were more or less on the same level; then, almost immediately, a great wall of water would rise between us and she would disappear from view. I watched as her hull and upper works vanished, then the derricks and Samson posts. It was frightening, but thrilling at the same time.

Conditions improved considerably on the afternoon of the fifth day, and we began to round up our convoy. They had been scattered far and wide.

We had been officially informed we would be going in for a refit after this trip, and – wonder of wonders – we were told where we would be going: somewhere on the Tyne.

A red-hot buzz went round the ship the day before we berthed: "We're paying off!"

"It's a fact," one of the stokers told us. "Got it from the canteen manager – Chief told him," he said. "Reckons he got it from the engineer officer!"

"The crafty bastards!" said Jim. "They never told us that."

It was rather sad in a way. We had been together for some considerable time; now it was time to pack our gear and say our goodbyes.

CHAPTER 9

BONNIE SCOTLAND (II): BONNIE LASSIE

She had blue eyes, fair, wavy hair parted in the middle, and a tip-tilted nose. In spite of the expression of reproval on her face as she looked up at me, I thought she was very pretty.

The expression on her face said, "You clot!" This was not surprising really, as not only had I bumped her when opening the door, but I was now walking all over the floor she had just washed.

'Bloody fool!' I thought. 'What do you think you're doing? You can see perfectly well it's sopping wet. Why didn't you go round the other side of the table? She hasn't done that side yet.' I wished I could have gone out and come in again, but it was too late now.

I carried on across the large kitchen to where four other girls stood in a group chatting.

"Pardon me," I said to the nearest one. "I'm to report to the chief cook."

"Are you a new helper?" she asked.

I nodded, and she said, "I'll go and tell Chief, but there's no need really. We can tell you what's what. I'm Helen," she added. "I'm supposed to be in charge of this lot – next to Chief, that is." She introduced the others: "Meg, Jessie and Barbara."

"Hello," I said, feeling more than a bit uncomfortable with four pairs of eyes weighing me up and another pair behind me.

'I wonder what her name is. She is a pretty little thing. Why did it have to be her I bumped into? Why couldn't it have been one of the others? I bet she won't want to know me. . . .'

My thoughts were interrupted by Helen's voice at the door: "The wee lass you nearly fell over is Jeannie."

I turned and said hello as she glanced briefly in my direction. I was not sure whether she answered or not.

There came the sound of voices and footsteps, and a large severe-looking woman in her forties, I guessed, strode into the room.

"So you are our new helper. I hope you're different to the last one they sent us. Surly, uncouth devil he was, and didn't want to know too much about work either!"

I said I would do what I could to help.

"Good," she replied. "Helen and the girls will look after you."

I had been late for the muster that Friday morning. 'Hands fall in' had just been piped, and I could not see my cap anywhere. After a frantic search I found it on the floor under the table.

'Some clumsy blighter must have knocked it down,' I thought, 'and couldn't be bothered to pick it up.'

I dashed outside, and fell in on the end of the line. The Petty Officer SDI gave me a scowl and went on detailing men off for various jobs. Some would be cleaning classrooms and offices, etc.; others would be handling stores, washing down paintwork or doing the odd bit of decorating. He paused as a chap came scurrying across from the guardroom and handed him a slip of paper.

He glanced at it and called out, "One hand to report to the Glentoran Hotel!" He turned and looked in my direction, and shouted, "You on the end, report to the Glentoran Hotel. Tell them you are a cook," he added. Then, to the remaining men: "The rest of you, clearing snow and ice."

I stood there mystified. Where and what was the Glentoran Hotel? And tell them I'm a cook? What the devil was he talking about?

The SDI turned back to me: "What are you hanging around for, then? See the lads in the guardroom – they will explain."

The killick (leading seaman) said, "You're a lucky sod –

Glentoran is down the other end of town. It's where the officers up here on courses are billeted – a nice quiet little number that, and there's a load of Wrens working there. Wouldn't mind going myself," he added. "Be more interesting than being stuck in here, I reckon."

"It sounds all right," I said, "but what's all this about telling them I'm a cook?"

"SDI's little joke that," he replied. "You'll be helping in the kitchen generally – opening tins, peeling spuds, washing up, etc. Anything that is going. This is what you do," he continued: "in about ten minutes' time the school bus will be going down to pick up the subbies for their day's courses. You can get a lift down on that each morning. Leave your station card in the office here, sign the 'Ashore on Duty' book, and sign in when you come back at night – OK?"

"How long is this job likely to last?" I asked.

"Can't answer that, chum," he replied. "Might be a few days only, or several weeks – depends how soon your draft comes through."

I made myself known to the bus driver, and was pleased to get a lift as there was quite a lot of snow and ice about.

I had been back at the base for about three weeks. My ship had 'paid off' at South Shields, as she was due for a very extensive refit. I had spent over two years on board her, and was rather sad to have to leave, as I think most of the lads were. Conditions on sloops were not at all bad. They were good sea boats, quite roomy, and we had been on the three-watch system. We all received ten days' leave, and then for the submarine-detector ratings it was back to our headquarters base in Scotland for disposal. The remainder of the crew would be going to HMS *Pembroke*, Chatham, which was our port division. I felt very sorry for them.

"Don't leave them in too long, or they will come out like marbles!" Jessie was telling me how to operate the potato-peeling machine. It stood close to the outside wall of the back kitchen. The machine consisted of an upright cylinder, with a rough-surfaced baseplate, which revolved quite fast and rubbed the skins off the potatoes.

"Put about half a bucketful in at a time," said Jessie, "and spin them for two or three minutes. Then let some water in to rinse them, and take them out by the little door at the bottom. You will soon get the hang of it. We take them inside then, and pick out any eyes with a knife. I should do about two bucketfuls each morning. If we should want any more, someone will let you know."

"Thank you," I said. "You are most helpful."

"That's all right," she replied. "Let's go back inside now and have a cup of tea. It's freezing out here." She smiled and added, "And when we've had our cup of tea, you can help me wash the breakfast things up."

I don't know how many people were billeted at the hotel, but there was a mountain of cups, saucers and plates, etc. However, the kitchen was well equipped and organised, so it was no problem really.

'I am going to like it here,' I thought.

There was just Jessie, Barbara and I present, and I wondered where the rest of the girls were.

Jessie answered my thoughts: "We work in shifts," she said. "Two will do breakfasts and afternoon teas in turn, while we all help with the main meals."

Barbara didn't talk much. She was a naturally quiet and placid kind of person, I thought. Jessie was a chatterbox, but very likeable.

"Have you been up here very long," she asked.

"About three weeks," I replied. "My ship 'paid off' at South Shields, and after ten days' leave I came back here for disposal."

She became quite excited and said, "I am from South Shields." Then she told me her home address, but I didn't know the place all that well.

Helen, Meg and Jeannie were Scots girls, she informed me, and then she asked me where I came from. When I told her

Newmarket, Suffolk, she exclaimed, "Oh, Mam Spam comes from Suffolk!" When I asked who Mam Spam was she replied, "She is the catering officer – we don't call her that to her face, though."

I thought it quite amusing.

Barbara left us when we had finished the washing-up, and I remarked how quiet she was. "That's probably why we are such good friends," said Jessie: "because I talk all the time. Barbara's dad is a parish priest," she went on. "Meg's dad has a textile business, and Jeannie's dad is a solicitor. My dad is just a welder in the shipyard."

"My father is just a gardener and general handyman, Jessie," I said, "but our fathers are both doing essential jobs, aren't they?"

"Helen's husband is in the merchant navy – she is the only married one of us. Are you married, Bill?"

"No," I replied.

"Helen and Mary work together – I don't think you have met Mary – and Meg and Jeannie are the other two. It's odd how opposites are drawn together," she went on. "Meg and Jeannie are very good friends. Meg is tall, dark and rather serious, while Jeannie is small, fair and a little bundle of fun."

"I don't think Jeannie was very pleased with me, Jessie – the way I came in, she probably thinks I'm an idiot."

"Oh, I shouldn't worry about that," she replied. "It was nothing really. You will like Jeannie when you get to know her, Bill."

"I doubt if I will have the chance," I replied, "judging by the look she gave me."

Jessie gave me a rather quizzical look, I thought, but didn't say any more. Our conversation ended there, and I went to work on the potatoes.

That first day passed quite quickly, and when I left in the late afternoon my head felt in a bit of a whirl. This was altogether different from the naval routine I had become so used to – no bugles or pipes, no falling in for this or that muster, etc.

'It's too good to be true,' I thought. 'I bet it doesn't last long.'

I felt unsettled all the weekend. My thoughts kept going over the events of Friday, and each time came back to the little fair-haired girl. She was so pretty, I thought. I hadn't sighted her any more during the day, and I wondered if she was not well. Another thought came into my mind: 'Maybe she has been drafted. I expect Wrens are sometimes moved around, just like we are. I hope not, because I wanted to see her again. For goodness' sake, forget it,' I said to myself. 'You caught a glimpse of a pretty face and are now behaving like a stupid schoolboy!'

I stayed on the base all weekend – washed some of my gear and darned some socks. It was a snug little place, this base. Prior to the navy taking it over, it had been a convalescent home, I believe. Basic naval routine was observed, but the whole atmosphere was completely different from that in the large barracks. I suppose any small community is friendlier than a larger one.

We slept in beds – only a few chaps to a room. A home from home, we thought!

I received a letter from home on a Saturday. The family were all well, and my mother told me she still continued to receive regular letters from my brother. He remained with 33 Squadron (Spitfires) throughout the war.

I myself wrote home regularly. I had left a numbered list with my family – place names with numbers – so they always had some idea of my movements. In each letter I included a sentence of some sort containing a number.

Our mail home was always censored, so there was no point putting in information which we knew would be struck out.

The war news was encouraging. The U-boat menace had been largely overcome, and there was constant speculation as to where we might be sent. We all crossed our fingers and hoped it would not be to the Far East. I was not too concerned at this prospect personally, as I had already done a spell of foreign service. In my simple reasoning, I thought perhaps they would not send me again!

Monday morning came, and I signed myself out and wondered what the day would bring. The school bus slipped and slithered its way along the streets, but we made it all right.

The sentry on our main gate had said to me, "You're a lucky bleeder – how did you manage to get a nice little number like that?"

"Just by accident," I replied.

"Anybody can have this job – I'll be a block of bleeding ice by the time I get relieved!" He looked and sounded pretty miserable.

It certainly was cold that morning – and it wasn't much warmer in the bus. It had been standing out in the open all night. I was pleased to get out of it and into the hotel.

I tapped lightly on the kitchen door, opened it – carefully this time – and went in. Two girls were busy washing up. I recognised Helen, but the other was a stranger. I said good morning to them, and Helen introduced the other girl.

"Meet Mary, Bill. We work together, and have been getting the breakfasts this morning."

I helped them finish the washing-up and had a cup of tea – there was always some tea or coffee going. Helen mentioned a few things I could do, and, of course, there would be the potatoes.

Mary was from Oldham and quite friendly, as most North Country people are. She had worked in a laundry, she informed me, before joining the Wrens. One or two of the other girls came into the kitchen while we were chatting, but there was no sign of Jeannie.

'Perhaps she has been drafted,' I thought – 'I hope not. Shall I ask Mary about her? No, I must not do that.'

I was feeling a bit sorry for myself as I put my overcoat on and went outside to the potato machine.

"Don't leave them in too long," Jessie had told me, and I soon found out what good advice that was.

The machine was a simple thing, but very efficient. I was pleased to get back inside again as it was still quite early, and very cold out there.

There was a smaller room at the back of the kitchen, and it was here I did the vegetable preparing, etc. It contained a table with a form at each side, and the girls had their meals there. I ate there too. After getting a bucket of water, I sat myself down and started picking eyes out. It was amazing how many potatoes a bucket held – especially if they were not very big.

An amusing thought came to me: 'If I grind them a bit longer in the machine, there won't be any eyes left to pick out! A bit naughty that – I don't think I will do that.'

Not a sound came from the kitchen.

'Perhaps the girls have all gone to make their beds, and tidy their rooms.' I thought how nice they all were, and contrasted their manners and conversation with that of the men on some of the mess decks I had been on at sea. Out there, every other word seemed to begin with F, and the main topic of conversation was about whores and 'bag shanties'.

The kitchen door was opened and closed a few minutes later, and I could hear voices and chuckling. I wondered who was in there, and was about to get up and show myself – I didn't want to eavesdrop – when the door was opened and closed again, and there was silence. No, I was mistaken – there was still someone there.

"Let him go, let him tarry, let him sink or let him swim."

Someone was singing softly to herself.

I sat quite still and listened.

"He doesn't care for me, and I don't care for him. Let him go and find—"

The kitchen door opened again, and the singer broke off. I could hear more voices and laughter.

'I really must show myself,' I thought, so I got up and walked through into the kitchen. My first reaction on seeing Jeannie was relief that she was still here – then apprehension. The other girl was Meg.

"Good morning," I said. "I hope I didn't startle you."

161

They both turned and replied. Meg smiled, but Jeannie looked a bit wary, I thought. Perhaps she was thinking, 'There is that clot again!'

"There is some tea in the pot if you would like some."

"Thank you, Meg," I said.

She poured a cup out and handed it to me. "Help yourself to milk and sugar."

The two girls continued their conversation, so I took my cup of tea out to the back room and sat down. A little while later I heard the kitchen door again – it became very quiet, and I assumed both girls had gone. I had just finished my first lot of potatoes, and I thought I had better put them in the kitchen and go out and start another lot.

Jeannie was alone – busy at one of the worktops. She turned her head when she heard me, and our eyes met.

"I bet you think I'm an oaf," I said.

"Do you?" she replied.

"That business when I came in on Friday – I'm sorry about that."

"I should think so indeed!" And she turned back to the worktops.

Was that all she was going to say? 'All right.' I thought. 'If that is your attitude, you can go to pot. I won't bother to say any more words to you.' But as soon as the thought came into my head I knew I did not mean it. I did not want to be 'bad friends' with any of the girls, least of all her. I felt rather hurt, resentful too, because I had not exactly committed a crime, had I?

The feeling passed, and I said, "I don't want us to be 'bad friends'."

She made no reply, and I asked, "Are you cross?"

She half turned her head as if to say something, and I thought just for a moment that she was trying very hard to conceal a smile – or did I imagine that?

Some of the other girls came into the room at that moment, so I went out.

'Better get some more potatoes, then,' I thought. 'I don't

want to have them shouting at me.'

What had Jessie called her – a little bundle of fun? Well, I was not feeling very amused.

'Not to worry, William,' I said to myself. 'Your name might be on the drafting board tonight. That will solve that little problem.' Somehow I didn't think I was very convincing.

"Hello, Bill."

I looked up to find Jessie standing there.

"Hello, Chatterbox," I replied.

"I've brought you a cup of coffee. And how are you today?"

"Oh, all right, Jessie, I suppose, thank you."

"Is there something wrong?" she asked.

"No, not really," I replied.

"Are you sure?" she said. "You look a bit down."

"It's nothing, Jessie. I am all right really."

"Jeannie is making some scones – would you like some, Bill?"

"Thank you," I said. "I tried to apologise to her just now, for the way I came in on Friday. She just said, 'I should think so,' and turned her back on me. I don't want to be 'bad friends' with any of you."

"I shouldn't worry about it," she replied. "There's probably a simple explanation."

"I don't understand," I said.

"I do," she replied. "I must get back now. I will bring you those scones in a minute."

I leaned back against the table and sipped my coffee, my thoughts wandering aimlessly: mealtimes in Chatham Barracks (the mad scramble to get a plate and knife and fork, and sometimes, when you did, the food could all be gone); the nightmare of those tunnels. I thought about the two burned seamen we had picked up. I remembered holding the arm of one of them while the ship's doctor peeled the charred skin off his palm and fingers, and his fingernails came away with it. How these poor men must have suffered! I tried to collect my thoughts. 'Back there in the kitchen just now, was she smiling at some secret joke or just laughing at me? I bet she thinks I'm an idiot.'

I was sitting staring at the floor when I realised I had company.

"I have brought you some scones – I hope you will like them."

"Thank you," I said, and looked up. "Oh, I thought it was Jess—" I broke off.

"Sorry to disappoint you," she said.

Was that a teasing little look in her eyes? I wanted to tell her I was not disappointed – that I was pleased it was her.

Instead I said, "I meant no, I didn't mean—" I broke off in confusion.

'What a muddle I'm getting into!' I thought.

She leaned slightly towards me, and, with an impish expression on her face, said, "Let's start again, shall we? I'm Jeannie – Jessie is the one with red hair!"

I felt such an idiot.

'Of course I know your name,' I thought. 'I have been thinking of you ever since Friday. You must think me a bigger idiot now than you did before. I want us to be friends, but everything seems to be going wrong.'

She sat down on the form close by. Her expression was serious now. Looking at me intently, she said, "Now tell me what is the matter."

"Nothing is the matter," I replied. "I am all right."

"I don't think you are," she said.

She looked rather concerned, I thought.

"Bill, are you worrying about what I said back there in the kitchen? Please don't. I was teasing you. It was very naughty of me – I am a little horror sometimes."

I couldn't think of anything to say.

She held out her hand and said, "I hope we will be good friends."

I thought again how pretty she was, and how nice.

"I'd better get back to work now – Chief is in the kitchen!"

"I should not have kept you," I said.

"I chose to stay," she replied with a smile, "but I must get back now." She made no attempt to get up, but smiled again and wriggled her fingers, and then I realised I was still holding her hand.

"Sorry," I said, and released it.

The impish expression returned to her face as she said, "Don't start apologising again, please, or we might get into another muddle!"

"No more muddles!" I said. "Thank you for coming, and for the scones – they look very nice."

She was about to leave when Chief came through the door.

"Good morning," she greeted me. "Are my girls looking after you all right?"

"Yes, thank you, Chief," I replied with my mouth full of scone.

"Good," she said; and turning to Jeannie she asked, "Did Helen give you my message?"

"Yes, Chief," Jeannie replied. "I can manage."

"Good girl." Then turning back to me she asked, "Do you get on all right with them?"

"Yes," I said, "they are nice girls, all of them."

"Good, I'm pleased you think so. I think the world of them – but, mind you, I would never let them know that."

She went on her way, and I thought, 'The girls are all a little bit scared of her, but she is an old softy really – like an old hen with her chicks.'

Jessie came through to see me a little later.

"I must say you are looking brighter than you were a little while ago – has Jeannie brought you some scones?"

"Yes, thank you, Jessie," I said. "Very nice they were too."

"I intended to myself," she said, "but I happened to be rather busy just then."

"I put my clumsy foot in it again, Jessie," I told her. "I thought she was you! We managed to get it sorted out all right, though," I added. I told her of our conversation, and she thought it quite amusing.

"Give her half a chance, Bill, and she will tease. It's just her innocent fun. She's sweet really, and we all love her."

"One little thing you said puzzled me, Jessie. Jeannie turning her back on me like that – what did you mean?"

"Oh," she replied, "I bet she was having a good laugh!"

She picked up my cup and plate and turned to go.

"Jessie."

"Yes?"

"Were you too busy really?"

She looked a bit sheepish, then said, "I couldn't leave you looking like that."

"You're kind and understanding," I said. "Thank you, Jessie."

"Girls, girls, girls! Have you all gone mad?" The smile on Chief's face belied her outraged manner. Turning to me, she said, "Look at the state of you! You had better take off that collar and dry it by the range. Somebody find him a towel."

I don't know whose idea it was to have a snowball fight, but two or three of the girls were outside by the potato store, and I could hear excited voices and laughter.

It was a few days later, and we had just finished washing up the lunch things. I liked this part of the day. We would tidy up the kitchen, and then there would be an easy spell for an hour or two. The girls would disappear – to change and tidy themselves up, I suppose. Some would return to the kitchen and sit reading, writing letters, or chatting together. There was a long wooden form at the side of the huge table, and we would sit there facing the cooking range. It was a really cosy spot.

Anyway, on this particular day I was sitting there reading one of the papers when Meg and Jeannie came bursting in – snow falling from their coats. They made a beeline for me – one coming round each end of the table.

"We want you!"

They hauled me to my feet, and, one on either arm, propelled me outside. There had been a quite heavy fall of snow the previous night, and it was snowing again now.

There was no doubt about who got the worst of it – my hair and collar were soaked! Three against one was not quite fair, but I didn't mind. I quite enjoyed it, in fact.

I think Chief brought us to our senses. I held the door as we trooped back in.

"Poor you!" Jeannie said as she passed me.

After getting myself dried off a bit, I sat down and a cup of tea was handed to me. Meg came and sat on one side of me, and Barbara the other a little distance away.

"It certainly is cold out there," she remarked.

"Yes," I said, "it's nice to get back inside."

We sat chatting together, and she told me she and her boyfriend were planning to get married on his next leave.

"What do you think about wartime marriages?" she asked.

"I really don't know, Barbara," I said. "I don't think I would want to – everything is so uncertain. The lads would often talk about it on the mess decks, and opinions seemed to be more or less equally divided, for and against. Some would say you should grab what happiness you can while you have the chance, and others would say it is a bit unkind to marry some nice girl, then go off and get yourself killed perhaps."

"Room for a small one?"

I had not realised Jeannie was back. She looked very neat and trim, and I thought how nice her hair was – I liked the way she did her hair. Her glance travelled the length of the form. Where was she going to sit, I wondered. I looked up and our eyes met.

"May I?" she asked.

I made a pretence of moving to my right (but I couldn't move really without coming close up against Meg) and she sat down.

Turning her head to face me, she said, "Are you all right now? It was very cruel of those girls."

"I am fine, thank you," I replied.

"We are pleased you came. We didn't like the last chap – he was horrible. You are much nicer."

"Thank you," I said.

"Do you like us?"

She was studying me very closely, I thought.

"I don't think I would meet any nicer girls anywhere," I said.

"Does that include me?" she asked, "because I am horrid really – I tease everybody."

"Yes," I said, "you too."

'How could any chap not like you?' I thought. 'You are a very pretty girl, have such a nice nature, and seem to radiate happiness.'

She smiled and said, "Is everything in place?"

I brought my eyes back to hers.

"I was thinking how nice your hair looks. I like the way you do it."

"Thank you," she replied. "Actually, I was thinking of changing it."

"Oh!" I said.

"You don't think I should?"

"I don't know," I replied. "I can't say that, can I?"

"Yes, you can," she said. "I don't mind – I was thinking of changing it to a side parting."

I tried to picture her hair with a side parting.

'It wouldn't look as nice,' I thought. 'It wouldn't suit her.'

"What do you think, then?" she asked.

"I'm sure it would look nice any way you did it." Evidently, I didn't sound very enthusiastic.

"You don't sound too sure," was her reply.

'What do I say to that?' I wondered. 'I'm beginning to get lost along the way.'

"Shall I change it, Bill, or keep it like it is?"

There was a broad smile on her face, and I thought, 'You are enjoying this, you little imp.'

I think Barbara was also – I noticed she was smiling.

"You must do it how you want it," I said. "It's not for me to say."

"I don't think he really cares how I have my hair," she said to the room at large, darting me an impish look from the corner of her eyes.

"It does look nice how it is," I offered.

I was not really sure if she was serious, or teasing me, but Meg came to the rescue. She put her hand on my arm and said, "I should strangle her, if I were you, Bill."

That remark caused general amusement.

'Thank you, Meg,' I thought. 'You have got me off the hook!'

"You wouldn't hurt me, would you?"

I turned back to Jeannie.

"Of course not," I said.

We were sitting very close – her shoulder resting on my upper arm.

'This is cosy,' I thought. 'I like it. I hope Barbara doesn't decide to get up.'

As it happened, she did, a minute or two later.

"I think I will go for a stroll, and post my letter," she said.

Meg left also, a little later.

Jeannie still sat as close to me, and I thought, 'I believe she really does like me.' I had wondered as much in the previous day or two, when she had smiled when I caught her eye as we had been working. I was certain that she knew I liked her.

Giving me a cheeky little look, she said, "I expect you are like all the sailors: girl in every port – that sort of thing!"

"I don't think so, Jeannie," I replied. "I don't have a girl in every port."

"Don't you like girls? Girls can be horrid sometimes." She turned her head to face me again. "What do you think, Bill?"

"I think you are a little imp who likes to tease," I said.

"What?"

"That's what Jessie told me you are!"

"Wait till I see Jessie!" she said.

We both laughed at that, and then we sat looking at each other.

'If I ask her out tonight, will she come?' I wondered. 'I would hate it if she said no.'

"Yes? You were going to say something?"

Her expression looked encouraging, I thought.

"Jeannie, I would like to ask you if we could meet after work."

She looked very thoughtful, then a smile appeared.

"Go on, then," she said. "I'm waiting." Her mood and expression changed now. "Do you think I am a scatterbrain, Bill? Do you think I am silly?"

"No," I replied. "I think you are ever so nice."

"You are beginning to understand me now?"

"I'm beginning to think I do," I said.

"You are nice to me, Bill."

"I find it very easy to be," I said.

I suddenly realised we were no longer alone – Meg was back in the kitchen.

"Would you two like a cup of tea?" she asked.

"Thank you, Meg," I replied.

She gave me a little smile and slowly raised her eyebrows.

"We had better start getting the teas, Jeannie. Time is getting on."

"What can I do to help, Meg?" I asked.

"You can slice some bread for us, please, if you will," she replied.

I busied myself at this, and after a while Jeannie called across to me and said, "I think you have forgotten something!"

"Forgotten something?" I repeated to myself. I couldn't for the life of me think what it could be. Was there some job or other I should have done and had not?

'Better concentrate on what you are doing, or you will be cutting your fingers instead of the bread,' I thought.

She came across to me a little later, and said, "I enjoyed our conversation – perhaps we can continue it later."

"You mean I can see you tonight?"

"If I seemed to suggest that," she replied, "it's just a coincidence!"

"One little thing bothers me a bit, Jeannie – it is very cold out there," I said.

"Have you changed your mind – are you wanting to put me off now?"

"No," I said. "I just meant there is nowhere much to go in town, and I wouldn't want you to get a chill or something, having become used to this nice warm place."

"We can go for a walk," she replied. "I will be all right."

"Jeannie."

"Yes?"

"What is it I have forgotten?"

"Oh," she replied, "you were going to ask me out. It has just occurred to me, Bill – I suppose you could wait here for me. It would save you having to walk right up there and back."

She didn't sound too sure, I thought.

"I appreciate your concern, Jeannie, but I'd better not – I don't think Chief would approve, would she?"

"No, perhaps not."

"Anyhow," I said, "I ought to go and see what's going on. And who knows, there might be some mail for me – but I doubt it!"

"I will walk to the door with you," she said when I left about half an hour later.

We were stopped in the hallway by a sub lieutenant. "Just a minute," he said, holding up his hand and giving me a sour look. "These are officers' quarters – what are you doing here?"

I didn't like his appearance, his manner or his tone. Neither did I like the way he looked at Jeannie.

"I am here on base authority," I said, "and will be every day until I am told different!"

"Oh!" he said, and turned and left us.

Jeannie's eyes followed him out of sight down the corridor.

"You pig!" she muttered.

"I didn't like the way he looked at you, Jeannie."

"Ignore him," she said. "He is the kind who thinks every girl should fall for him – those that don't suffer in other ways!"

"You mean he has been pestering you?" I asked.

"He has tried it on with several of the girls," she replied.

"You must make a complaint to Chief or Mam Spam, Jeannie," I said. "They will soon put a stop to it," I said.

"You sound very cross, Bill. I haven't seen you cross before."

"That pig!" I said.

"Forget him, Bill – we girls can deal with the likes of him." She smiled and said softly, "I believe you care."

I quickly scanned the noticeboard when I arrived back at the base, and I breathed a sigh of relief when I didn't see my name there.

'I hope it will not be for a long time,' I thought.

A chorus of cheers greeted me when I entered my room.

"The wanderer returns," said Allan Clarke, who was a special friend of mine.

"He likes to come and give us a look now and again," said another voice.

"Mystery bloke you are, Matt – you disappear every morning and reappear at night. Where the hell do you go to all day?"

"You got some secret hiding place somewhere?" asked another lad.

"Yes," I replied, "you could call it that."

They gave me some blank looks, so I thought I'd better tell them what I was doing.

"You lucky sod!" one of them exclaimed. "How did you manage to get a job like that?"

"Because one of you lot knocked my hat down one morning," I said, "and I was too bloody lazy to pick it up."

They gave me some odd looks, but I didn't say any more.

"Got it made, haven't you? Lucky bastard!"

Bernie Taylor spoke the words. He was an offensive, dirty-minded character – none of us liked him.

"All them tarts down there – how many are there?"

"None," I said, "but there are six very nice and respectable girls."

"Huh – they're all the bloody same, ain't they?"

"No," I replied, "there is all the difference in the world; but, of course, a dirty slob like you wouldn't appreciate that – the only kind you know about are waterfront whores!"

I was getting a bit worked up, and I thought, 'If he says much more, I'm going to land him one.'

"Calm down, Matt," said Allan. "We all know how the dirty sod thinks – ignore him; he's not worth it."

"He had better watch it, Allan," I said. "They are nice girls he's talking about."

"Bernie wouldn't know a decent party if he saw one," remarked one of the others.

"What's so bloody special about them, I'd like to know? You ain't going to tell me he ain't had it off with them."

"Shut your trap, Bernie," said someone, "and get back in the gutter with your whores – that's where you belong!"

"Ought to be me working down there. Reckon I could do all of them a bit of good."

That did it. The thought of the likes of him touching Jeannie, or any other girl for that matter, was too much. I turned and hit him in the middle of his face, and went for him again.

"That's enough!" The room's leading hand stepped in.

"You got what you asked for, Taylor," he said. "Serves you bloody right!"

He turned to me, winked and said, "No fighting on the mess deck!"

"That should quieten him down, Matt – I was itching to hit him myself," said Allan. "I wouldn't let the dirty bastard within half a mile of my sister," he added. "I hope he doesn't get the same ship as me. Tell us about the girls, Matt – what are they like?"

I described them, and said what a nice lot they were. "Mary is going out with one of the lads from the base here, apparently. She told me his name, but I don't know him."

We chatted for another ten minutes or so, then I noticed the time by the clock on the wall of our room.

"It's time I was getting ready, Allan," I said.

"Going ashore, Matt?" he asked. "Anywhere special?"

"I'm going to see one of my mates, Allan – one of my workmates," I added.

He looked rather puzzled, then smiled. "I get it, Matt – very nice too!"

"Yes, Allan," I replied, "she is."

I watched her come down the drive, through the entrance gates and across the road to where I was waiting.

"Hello. How smart you look!" I said. "I haven't seen you with your hat on before."

"Hello," she replied. "Are you pleased to see me?"

"Yes, Jeannie, I am."

"I am you too," she replied.

She slipped her arm through mine, and we started off.

"Where shall we go?" she asked.

"You lead the way," I said. "I am a foreigner in these parts."

"Sassenach," she replied, "that's what you are!" She laughed and squeezed my arm. "Was there any mail for you?"

"No, nothing," I replied. "I don't get many letters – just from my mother and sister."

"Nothing from those two girls?" she asked.

"No – they don't write to me, Jeannie."

"Why not?" she asked.

I laughed and said, "Because I don't write to them, I expect."

"Don't you like them, Bill?"

"Yes, they are all right," I said. "We are just friends, nothing more."

The previous two or three mornings Jeannie had brought my coffee – her own as well – and we had sat and talked. She had asked me if I had a girlfriend at home. I told her that I didn't, but I was friendly with two girls I had grown up with who lived nearby.

"How convenient!" she had said.

"We are just friends from childhood, nothing more."

We had walked some considerable distance by now. It was very cold, and a few flakes of snow had begun to fall. I had no idea where we were, and wasn't even sure which direction we were going in.

"I was thinking how lucky I am having this job, Jeannie," I remarked. "Mary's friend only sees her in the evenings – I am with you all day."

"However can you bear it!" she said. "Those two girls – tell me about them."

"Not much to tell, Jeannie, really. As I said, we sort of grew up together."

"What do they look like?" she asked.

"One has brown hair and is a little taller than you; the other has black hair and a dark complexion."

"She sounds glamorous and mysterious. Do you like her best, Bill?"

I hesitated. 'I am getting a bit hemmed,' I thought.

174

"Yes!" I laughed and said, "Both girls are just friends. Do you have anyone, Jeannie?"

"There was a boy I was friendly with," she replied, "but we haven't seen each other for some time now – we were just good friends."

"When I have to leave, Jeannie, can we keep in touch – will you write to me?"

"Yes, and you to me. I would like that. Do you think you might be leaving soon, Bill?"

"I really don't know," I said. "I haven't heard anything, but I suppose I could at any time. I hope it will not be yet."

"I do also. We get on so well together, don't we?"

"Yes, we do," I replied.

We walked on in silence for a bit. It had stopped snowing. There was bright starlight now and a nearly full moon. The cold was becoming intense. My ears were tingling, and the fresh snow was crisp under our feet.

"Are you all right, Jeannie – not frozen?" I asked.

"I am a bit cold," she replied. "Let us step out a bit."

We had been dawdling along, and I was none too warm myself.

"We will soon be back," I said. "Then you can make a hot drink to warm you up."

"I would like to ask you in, Bill – we could both have one – but I'm not sure if I should."

"A kind thought," I said, "but we must not do that, must we? Anyway, I'd better be getting back to the base pretty soon or I will be adrift [AWOL]. A comical thought just came into my head, Jeannie: I pictured us sitting in the kitchen having a cup of cocoa, and that pig of an officer walked in. I expect he would say, 'What, you again! Do you work here twenty-four hours a day?'"

She was highly amused.

"May I see you in the morning – say about eight o'clock?"

"I will be expecting you," she replied. "You will be just in time to wash the breakfast things up for me!"

We parted.

On arrival back at the base, I made my nightly check of the

noticeboard. My name was not to be seen, I was pleased to note. My room-mates seemed in high spirits when I went in.

"Is it somebody's birthday?" I asked.

"No, Matt – but we are celebrating."

"Why – what's happened?" I asked.

"That dirty sod Taylor – he's going. Didn't you check the board when you came in? A new list went up tonight."

"I did," I said, "but I only looked for my own name."

"I reckon he volunteered," said Allan. "Thought somebody else might thump him!"

"Anyhow – bloody good riddance, I say."

It was the end of a perfect day, I thought.

"What do you think of Scotland – do you like it?"

"I haven't seen much of your country," I replied, "just this part where our two bases are. I thought the scenery was great around our training base. I was there for about two months in the summer of '42, and the weather was perfect."

We were having our 10 a.m. coffee break the next day.

"Perhaps one day I will have a car and go on a tour around Scotland," I said. "Have you ever been to my part of the country, Jeannie?"

"No, I haven't," she replied.

"You would find it rather flat, I think, although there are gentle hills and valleys in some parts."

"Mam Spam comes from your county, Bill, but I don't know where exactly."

"I like the nickname, Jeannie – who gave her that?"

"I don't know," she replied. "We have to call Wren officers ma'am, so perhaps it evolved naturally, so to speak."

"I notice you haven't changed your hair yet."

"I am not going to, Bill."

"Oh, you have changed your mind?"

"No, I was just teasing you yesterday – I wondered what you would say!"

"I was a bit confused," I said. "I thought you were serious at first, and then I wasn't sure."

"You must think I am awful, Bill."

"No, I don't," I replied; "I think you are ever so nice."

"I think you are too," she said.

Sounds of activity came from the kitchen.

"Time to start work again, Bill." She smiled across at me as she got up. "I will join you for lunch if I may."

"I would like that," I replied, "then perhaps we could have afternoon tea together also!"

We did just that, in the cosy spot, leaning back against the kitchen table.

Helen asked if she could have the paper when we had finished with it. "I'm sure I don't know when that will be," she said. "You have been turned to that page for the last twenty minutes. You both must be very slow readers!" She gave us a kindly smile when she said it, but she knew, I think, that we were pretending to read the paper, in order to conceal the fact that we were holding hands.

I handed it to her. "Sorry, Helen – you should have said."

"That's all right," she replied. "I will take it to my room and leave you in peace." She smiled at us again, and left.

"I think Scottish girls are very nice, Jeannie."

"Oh, have you known a lot?"

"No," I said, "just you, Helen and Meg. Oh, and there were two I met at our training base."

"You have two girlfriends down there, Bill?"

"No, I didn't say that." I laughed and said, "I just met two girls there. I only saw them a couple of times," I added.

"Were they nice – were they pretty?"

"I don't really know – they were all right, I suppose."

"Didn't you notice – or perhaps you have forgotten. What were their names, Bill?"

"I don't remember," I said. "It was nearly three years ago. They were not local girls – just there on holiday for a few days."

"Where were they from, Bill?"

"I don't remember that either," I replied.

"You're not sure whether you knew them or not!"

I turned my head to look at her. She was smiling broadly.

"You little tinker!" I said. "What am I going to do with you! We will try and be serious now. When I was at our training base I was good friends with a lad named Harry Thomas – 'Tommo' we called him. He was from Nottingham. We used to go ashore together, and we went for walks in the hills quite often. We must have walked miles sometimes. Anyway, we were strolling through the town one evening when Tommo said, 'Look at those two parties over there – I think they want us to go and say hello.' Parties, Jeannie, are what sailors call girls. A pretty girl would be a smashing party."

"I wish I were a smashing party, Bill." She was attempting to look very sorrowful.

"You *are* a smashing party," I said: "an extra-smashing party – a bonnie lassie!"

"I'm not really, but I'm pleased you think so, Bill."

The kitchen door was opened, and Chief came into the room. She held some papers in her hand, and she pinned them on the small board on the wall.

Coming towards us, she said, "Good afternoon – you are still with us, I see. Do you like it here?"

"Yes, Chief," I replied. "It is a welcome change from the normal routine – and nice people."

"Good!" she said. "You have been a good help to my girls, I hear, and you seem to be well liked."

I thought there was the faint suspicion of a smile on her face as she went out.

"Where did I get to, Jeannie?"

"You were telling me about your two girlfriends!"

"Please don't let us start that again," I said. "My inside still hurts from laughing. Briefly, Tommo and I went for a couple of walks with these girls, the second of which was quite amusing, I recall – well, we thought so afterwards. We were going through a farmyard where there was a flock of geese. They began cackling and flapping their wings, then they came for us and we ran for it! It was a bit alarming at the time. I will look forward to Monday morning," I said.

It was late afternoon on the Friday, and we were saying

goodbye at the door. It didn't seem possible I had been there a whole week.

"How will you spend your weekend, Bill?" she asked.

"I shall stay on the base, I expect – I may wash some of my things out," I replied.

"Won't you go out with some of your friends on Saturday evening? You may meet up with some more nice Scots girls!"

"After the muddle I got into with those other two, I hope I don't," I said.

"Don't you like them any more?"

"Just this one," I said, "but I must be off soon, and let you get ready. I hope you have a nice weekend – your parents will be pleased to see you."

"Thank you. I am lucky to be based so near my home. You are a long way from yours, Bill."

"It was worse when I was based at Londonderry, Jeannie. I would leave my ship about lunchtime, and wouldn't get home sometimes until late evening the following day. It was very tiring, with the delays and diversions, and the trains being so crowded. See you on Monday morning."

It seemed strange to be back at the base for two whole days – something like going back to work after being on holiday. I felt I was living two separate lives: in one there was a pleasant atmosphere, nice people and a complete absence of authority; in the other there were the continual pipes and orders coming over the Tannoy, the frequent arguments among the blokes, and the eternal cursing and swearing. I couldn't remember hearing one swear word from the girls since I had been there. I had nearly let something slip myself a couple of times. At sea everyone on the mess decks cursed almost all the time – one another, the officers, the ship, the food, the ocean, the Germans and the war – just about everything we could think of.

I knew I could be going back to it all at any time, and the thought depressed me. I think we had all had enough of it by now. The end of hostilities couldn't come soon enough.

Things were pretty quiet now for the navy. In home waters

and the Atlantic the U-boats had been decisively beaten, and the Mediterranean too was safe for shipping once more. I felt sure we would be sent to the Far East, and I hoped we wouldn't encounter too many of those kamikazes!

'Maybe the war won't last much longer,' I told myself. 'This could very well be my last stay at this base. When it is all over I'll probably be going back to Chatham Barracks for demob. When I do go from here, will I ever see Jeannie again? I do hope we keep in touch, and that we can meet again one day. Perhaps, after the war, she will invite me to come and see her. On second thoughts, though, would she want me to? She will be back among her friends, and no doubt we will be moving in different circles.' I did not know what to think.

Monday morning came again, and I signed myself out.

Jessie and Barbara were in the kitchen when I arrived. They seemed pleased to see me, as I was them – Jessie especially. I had a soft spot for Chatterbox, as I called her, and regarded her as my confidante. We had a little chat and a cup of coffee, and then set to work.

I was busy outside a little later, churning some potatoes, when I heard Jeannie's voice at the doorway behind me.

"Bill, I was so worried about you!"

I turned and walked the few steps towards her. She looked worried, I thought.

"Hello, Jeannie. What is the matter?"

"I came down," she replied, "and there was no sign of you. I thought you had gone."

"I wouldn't leave without letting you know – somehow or other," I said.

"I came and looked out here, but couldn't see you, Bill – and your coat was not there!"

"Poor you!" I replied. "I was probably in the potato store. Cheer up – they are not going to send me away yet, Jeannie. I told them I was needed down here – that Chief needed me to keep her girls in order. Not to mention that there was a mountain of spuds to be peeled!"

Smiling now, she asked, "And what did they say to that?"

"Oh, we understand, Bill – you stay as long as you like!"

We both laughed at that.

'I wish they would say that,' I thought.

"Thank you for being concerned, Jeannie. Now don't get cold – it's freezing out here. See you at coffee time."

"Yes, all right," she replied; then, smiling broadly, she said, "I don't want to alarm you, but your machine is still going – there will be nothing left of them!"

"Good heavens," I said, "I had forgotten all about it!"

I dashed to the machine and switched it off. What would they be like? I wondered. They were just as Jessie said they would be: marbles!

'Not to worry!' I thought. 'There's plenty more where they came from.'

The time arrived, and we had our chat.

"Did you enjoy your weekend?" I asked.

"Yes, thank you."

"It seems ages since we said goodbye on Friday, Jeannie."

"You missed me?"

"Very much," I replied.

"I did you too, Bill. How did you spend your weekend after all?"

'I will pull her leg a bit,' I thought.

Putting on what I hoped was a serious face, I said, "I decided to go ashore after all on Saturday evening, with my friend Allan."

"Oh, did you?" she said.

"We went to the dance – Allan likes to go dancing. I'm not all that fond of it myself, but it turned out to be a really pleasant evening."

There was a puzzled expression on her face as she asked, "How do you mean, Bill?"

"Well," I said, "you remember pulling my leg on Friday about meeting some nice girls? Well, we actually did get into conversation with two. I walked one of them home afterwards."

She went very quiet for a full minute or more, then asked,

"Will you be seeing her again?"

'That's enough,' I thought. 'Joke's over.'

"Jeannie."

"Yes?"

"I am a terrible liar. I didn't meet any girls – I stayed on the base all weekend!"

"You were teasing me?"

"Yes, Jeannie."

"You little devil!" she said.

"It must be contagious, Jeannie, this teasing business."

"Who was Gordon, Bill?"

Meg asked me the question. It was a day or two later, and we were doing the breakfast washing-up together. She had been quite talkative; I was surprised, as she had always seemed rather quiet and serious. It began with her asking me what I did before the war.

"Nothing very exciting, Meg," I replied. "I worked on a farm – I left elementary school at the age of fourteen, and started work the next day. Times were hard, and I was expected to start bringing some money home."

She looked very thoughtful then said, "I am very fortunate, Bill. Daddy has a business, and I have been lucky enough to have had what you would call a good education. I don't know what it is to want for anything. Joining the Wrens is the only useful thing I have done – I don't know what I will do after the war."

"I don't think any of us will know quite where we are when the war is over, Meg. Everything seems upside down. People get thrown together, then separated again. I suppose it is good to meet new people, but it's sad sometimes when we have to leave them again."

"I have often thought how awful it must be for the married ones, Bill. They are often separated for long periods, and must all the time wonder if they will ever see each other again."

"I have thought that too," I said. It was then I told her about Gordon: "We were on those terrible Malta convoys together.

182

We lost no end of men and ships out there, and we were all convinced we would never come home again. Gordon's wife must have known, or guessed, he was out there. How she must have dreaded those announcements on the radio whenever a ship was sunk: 'The Admiralty regrets . . .'! A few days after I left that ship, Meg, she was torpedoed and sunk. If they had been at action stations when it happened, Gordon is unlikely to have made it."

"Oh, the poor boy!" she said.

The kitchen door opened and Jeannie came in.

"I hope you two are not thinking I'm shirking my duties," she remarked. "I will be back in a minute – Jessie and I have decided to change rooms."

"She's very fond of you, Bill," Meg said when she had gone.

"I think a lot of her too," I replied. "It worries me a bit sometimes."

Jeannie was back a minute or two later, and she came and stood between us.

"Oh dear," she said. "Looks like I am too late – you have nearly finished!"

"Never mind," I said.

"You can make us all a cup of coffee," said Meg.

I watched her as she did so, and thought how happy and carefree she looked. How awful it would be if someone she loved was trapped in the bottom of a ship as it went down! I quickly shut the picture out – I couldn't bear the thought of Jeannie grieving.

About two hours later we had our usual coffee break and chat. We had arranged to meet that evening and go for another walk.

"We must not dawdle along too much," I said, "or we will get frozen again."

"I will put a thick woolly on," she replied.

"I think I will too, Jeannie," I said. "I just hope I can get my jumper over it!"

"You could dress as normal, Bill, and put the woolly over

your jumper – no one would know, with your overcoat on."

"That's a good idea, Jeannie," I said, "but I'm not sure if I would be able to get my overcoat on then!"

We both began laughing.

"We seem to be getting into a muddle," she said. "Let's talk about something else. Meg was telling me about that poor boy on your ship, Bill."

"I only hope he got off all right, Jeannie."

She looked at me with a thoughtful expression on her face, and remarked, "You were lucky, Bill."

"Yes," I replied. "Apparently my number hasn't been called yet. That's what I thought when I heard the news."

"Please don't talk like that," she said.

"I'm sorry, Jeannie, but that was how we used to think out there. They were terrible times, and I would not want to go through it all again. It is all in the past now – and best forgotten, I think. Anyway, I had to be spared so I could come and see you! Sorry," I added: "that was supposed to be a joke. We nearly did not meet, Jeannie – it was only by accident."

I was about to explain, when Helen spoke from the doorway: "When you have finished your coffee, Jeannie, could you come and help us?" She was smiling when she said it.

"I must go, Bill. However long have we been sitting here?"

I leaned back on the form, so I could see the clock on the kitchen wall through the open door.

"I'm not quite sure what time you brought the coffee, Jeannie, but I should say at least three-quarters of an hour."

"Good heavens!" she exclaimed. "They will throw me out of the service!"

"What did you mean, Bill – only by accident?"

We sat in the cosy spot again.

I told her about the Friday morning, when I was late on parade. "I hope to find out who knocked my hat down, Jeannie, so I can thank him!" I told her also about another time I was a bit late falling in and thought I was going to drown in the swimming pool.

"How awful!" she said. "Whatever were they thinking about?"

"Teaching me to swim," I replied, "the fast way!"

We met again in the evening, and went for another walk.

"I am curious," she said: "when you first saw me, what did you think?"

"How pretty you were," I replied.

"Really, Bill?"

"Yes, Jeannie. I think you are a lovely girl. I like your nature, and your sense of humour is great – I have never met anyone quite like you."

"You say the nicest things," she said.

I thought back to that Friday morning when I walked into the kitchen and saw her for the first time. That was exactly what I had thought – how pretty she was. The other thing that struck me, when I bumped her leg with the door, was that she had a hole in her stocking! There is nothing odd about that really – I suppose we all get holes in our socks, and stockings. I always seemed to be mending mine. Perhaps I should have thrown more old ones away and bought new ones! I didn't mind really, though – it helped to pass the time and occupy my mind.

'Shall I tell her,' I thought, 'and see what her reaction is?' The thought amused me.

"May I share your joke?" she asked.

I turned and looked at her. "I'm not sure if I should tell you," I said.

"Why – is it awful?"

"No, Jeannie, not awful, but it may embarrass you."

"Sounds very intriguing. Whatever is it?" she asked. We had come to a halt, and were standing face-to-face. "I am all ears. Tell me, Bill."

"All right Jeannie. I told you the first thing I noticed about you; now I will tell you something else I noticed."

"My knees feel weak," she said.

"I'd better hold you closer – so you don't fall down!" I began to laugh – I couldn't help it.

"Whatever are you going to say, Bill?"

"Nothing really – just that you had a hole in your stocking."

"Oh!" she exclaimed. Then she stamped her foot and said, "How very romantic!"

We both laughed at that.

"It was probably one of many," she said. "I wear any old stockings for work."

"I understand, Jeannie. You didn't mind?"

"No, of course not, silly."

"There was a chap on my last ship", I said, "who would never wash or mend any of his socks."

"What did he do, then," she asked, "just keep throwing them away?"

"No, Jeannie, he kept piling them in his locker, and when he went home on leave he took them with him for his wife to do."

"She should have refused."

"That is what we used to tell him, Jeannie."

We walked on in silence for a bit.

"We seem to have exhausted the subject of socks and stockings."

"Yes, Jeannie. Let's talk about something else."

"Do you have some nice friends on the base, Bill?"

"Yes," I replied. "There is my special friend Allan, and two or three others in my room are nice lads. There was one nasty type, but he has just been drafted."

"Didn't you like him, Bill?"

"None of us did, Jeannie. I'm glad they sent me down to help you girls, and didn't send him; he thought all girls were tarts. I hope they send a decent chap in my place when I go. Jeannie."

"Yes." We had come to a halt again. "What is it, Bill?" she asked.

"When I go, Jeannie, I don't want you to worry about me."

"What do you mean, Bill – of course I will be concerned."

"Think of me sometimes, please," I said, "but don't worry about me."

I felt sick, thinking about leaving.

"I will miss you very much," she said.

"I will you too, Jeannie, but maybe I will have a bit longer yet. How long have other helpers stayed?"

"The previous one – the one we didn't like – stayed just a week or so, but I wouldn't take too much notice of that. Chief rang your base and told them he was no use to us. The one before him stayed about a month, as far as I remember."

We turned and started on our way back again.

"What will you do after the war, Bill?"

"I don't know," I said. "I haven't given it much thought really. I don't have any idea what I want to do. I did wonder, earlier on, if I might re-enlist in the navy, but everything is so uncertain; the war is not over yet."

"Wars are very cruel, Bill – they bring people together, and then part them again."

"Yes," I replied. "If it had not been for the war, I don't suppose we would have ever met, would we?"

"No, I suppose not. When you come home, Bill, will we see each other again?"

"I hope so, Jeannie. We will keep in touch, won't we?"

"Yes, we must."

We had been back at our meeting place some time now, and I thought it must be getting pretty late. I didn't want to be adrift and get my leave stopped for several days.

"We had better say goodnight now, Jeannie. I will be down to see you in the morning – perhaps you will have coffee ready."

"I hope your boss will be on time!" she said.

We went for more walks over the next week or so; then, on a Wednesday night, the blow fell.

For some reason I did not check the noticeboard on my arrival back at base, and on entering my room I was greeted by Allan's excited voice: "Great news, Matt!"

I looked at him blankly.

"Haven't you seen the noticeboard?" he asked. "We've got the same ship! She's down in Chatham Dockyard – heavy cruiser. We're joining her on Friday."

My brain barely took in what he was saying.

"They have been calling you over the Tannoy, Matt. I went and told them where you were. We have to report to the drafting office in the morning."

I felt sick and numb. My little world seemed to be collapsing. What had Allan said? Report to the drafting office in the morning? That means I won't be going down there any more. I won't see her again – not even to say goodbye.

I vaguely heard Allan's voice again: "Ted says they are all right – he's served on one of that class. Are you listening, Matt? What's the matter with you – having a dream or something?"

"No, Allan," I replied, "a nightmare."

He looked at me oddly. "You all right?" he asked. He walked across the room and joined me. "What's the trouble, old mate?"

I told him about Jeannie.

"This bloody war!" he muttered. "It is worse still when you are married, Matt – every time I say goodbye to my wife it tears me apart. Not to worry!" he went on. "We are not leaving until sometime on Friday. We are watch ashore again tomorrow night – you will be able to see her then. Anyway, I'm pleased we have got the same ship." He gave a little smile and said, "We'll be able to cry on each other's shoulders!"

I sat down and tried to collect my thoughts: 'Must get a message to Jeannie – tell her I will be late in the morning. I suppose I could ring the hotel from the guardroom now, but it's rather late. I will write a note for the bus driver to take when he goes down, and then, when I'm finished at the drafting office, I will go down and see her. If they want me back here, they will have to send for me.'

Allan was talking again: "You and her, Matt – is it serious?"

"I don't quite know how to answer that," I replied.

"You think a lot of her?"

"Yes, I do," I said.

"How about her, Matt?"

"I think she likes me a lot, Allan," I said.

"Bloody war!" he repeated.

"You are a good mate, Allan. I am pleased we are going to the same ship."

I hardly slept that night, and was not sorry when reveille was sounded. "Report to the drafting office," Allan had said, but first things first: go and find the bus driver – the lads in the guardroom will know which is his room.

I soon found him, and gave him my note.

"Leave it to me," he said. "I'll see she gets it all right. I bet you are sorry you're losing that little job."

"Yes," I replied.

"Bloody war!" he muttered.

The drafting routine didn't take very long, and I set out for the hotel. Nobody had told me I was finished down there, so I carried on as normal.

Jessie and Barbara were in the kitchen when I arrived. I told them my draft had come through, but I think they already knew.

"We shall all miss you, Bill," Jessie said.

"I will miss you girls too," I replied. "I have enjoyed being here, and it has been a pleasure knowing you all."

Jeannie came through to see me a minute or two later. She looked very sad.

"You are going, Bill?"

"Yes, Jeannie. It had to come, didn't it?"

We sat down in silence. Oh, to put the clock back! Looking across the table at her, I thought, 'You will never know how much I am going to miss you.'

We went for our last walk that evening, round by the loch side. We didn't talk very much – it all seemed so different now. I don't know how far we walked, but it seemed an eternity before we arrived back at our meeting place.

"It must be ever so late, Jeannie. Will you be able to get in all right?"

"Yes," she replied. "I asked Helen to leave the door unlocked for me. Will you get into trouble, Bill?"

189

"No," I said. "I will be all right. I will always remember these last few weeks, Jeannie."

"I will also," she replied. "It has been so nice."

We were two young people the war had brought together; now the war was about to part us again.

"It has been a lovely friendship, Bill."

"Yes, Jeannie. Whatever happens in the future, no one can ever take that away, can they?"

"No." The reply was barely a whisper.

"It must be nearly midnight, Jeannie. We will have to go. Goodbye, little girl. You never know – they might send me to another place to help one day and you will be there. Goodbye."

I watched her safely in, and, with a heavy heart, turned to make my way back to base.

'Will I ever see her again,' I wondered, 'or was it a final goodbye we just said? It must be hellish late – I'm well adrift for sure. I shall be in the rattle in the morning. To hell with them! Let them do what they like!' At that moment I couldn't have cared less. 'So why am I hurrying? Slow down – might as well be hung for a sheep as for a lamb.'

"You thought you would come back, then!" That was the greeting I got from the sentry on the gate.

And from the killick in the guardroom: "Where the bloody hell have you been? Do you know what the time is?"

"No," I replied.

"It's quarter past bleeding twelve," he snapped, "that's what it is!" He thrust my station card into my hand. "Here, grab hold of this. I have signed you in – you'd better get out of sight pretty sharpish, and think yourself bloody lucky!"

I thanked him, and he replied, "It's OK, but you want to watch it!"

"Yes," I said, "I will."

We left the next afternoon – a party of six of us. Allan and I made the long journey down to Chatham; two of the other lads were going to Hull to join a corvette; and I don't remember where the remaining two were going.

Standing on the little wooden landing stage, waiting for the ferry, I thought, 'Will I ever come back to this place again?'

The previous few weeks had been so pleasant; the war had seemed years away. It had been a welcome break after nearly two and a half years on Atlantic convoys. Now we were about to become involved with the Japanese, and there was no telling what that might mean.

"What are you thinking about, Matt?" asked one of the Hull-bound lads. "You looked bloody miles away just now."

"I was wondering if any of us will ever come back here again, Ron," I said.

"Cheerful bleeder you are!" he retorted. "I've got through the war this far – I ain't aiming to get killed now!"

"I didn't mean it that way," I said. "If the war ends when we are out East, we won't be coming back here, will we? It will be to our main barracks for demob."

"Horrible depressing thought!" said one of the others. "Chatham bloody gaol! I never want to see that place again! Lost half my kit there," he went on. "Thieving bastards – I couldn't trust anybody."

"I reckon we all feel the same about *Pembroke*," said Allan, "but I'll put up with it for a few days to get my demob."

One of the others, a Londoner, spoke for the first time: "I have got a little bit of business to attend to in Chatham Barracks."

We all looked at him and waited.

"Yeah," he went on, "a certain chief petty officer – one of that bloody Gestapo crowd! When I'm finished with that demob routine, I'm going to wait outside the *Pembroke* main gate, and when that bastard comes ashore I'm going to fill his bloody face in!"

He looked as though he meant what he said.

"I've heard it said", remarked Allan, "that none of that lot ever goes ashore – they are too bloody scared to."

"I wonder how much longer the war will last," I said. "I think the Germans have nearly had it – I don't know about the Japs."

"Could take years to clear them bleeders out," said the Londoner.

"It's being so cheerful that keeps you going, Alf," remarked his mate.

The little ferry boat came alongside and made fast, and we dumped our kitbags and hammocks on board. I turned back for a last look.

"Come on, Matt – it's time to go."

I jumped down into the boat, beside Allan.

"You will be coming back here!" he said.

"I doubt it, Allan," I replied, and, in response to his puzzled expression, added, "She doesn't live here, Allan; her home is about 100 miles from here."

"I should have known that, Matt. Nobody ever gets based in their own hometown, do they?"

When the boat was about halfway across, I thought to myself, 'If it was not so murky, I would be able to see the Glentoran from here,' but the whole coastline was just a blur. 'Maybe it is just as well,' I thought.

CHAPTER 10

OUT EAST

After my previous ship, this one seemed immense: a heavy cruiser of 10,000 tons, and a crew of about 1,100 men. We learned she had been in Chatham Dockyard for about six months and had just had an extensive refit. Her main armament had originally consisted of eight eight-inch guns, in four twin turrets, but 'X' turret was removed at this time to make room for more AA weapons. Secondary armament was eight four-inch guns in twin turrets, and she now had a heavy AA armament consisting of forty-eight two-pounder pom-poms, in six eight-gun mountings, plus a score or more of twenty-mm Oerlikons. The eight-barrel pom-pom was a fearsome close-range weapon, and could deliver half a ton of shells per minute. This gun was reckoned to be the best defence against dive-bombers.

We asdic operators were not at all happy when shown the location of our operating cabouche. It was on the deck below the mess deck, up in the forepart of the ship, next to the paint store – a depressing place.

Now the last of the stores and provisions were being brought on board – another day or two and we would be on our way. Exactly where we would be heading for was anybody's guess. We were all agreed it was definitely to the Far East – somewhere.

"Maybe we will end up in the Pacific," suggested someone, "helping them goddam Yanks out!"

"They were a long time deciding to come and help us out," came a reply.

"I remember my father saying the same thing about the First World War," I said.

"I guess we've come to finish the goddam war for you."

"You've been a bloody long time thinking about it!"

"Must have been terrible, the First World War," said Allan: "all that trench warfare – thousands of blokes mown down by machine guns or blown to bits. My old chap was in that first big push on the Somme – walking straight into massed machine-gun fire. Blokes were falling all around him, like ninepins. He used to break out in a sweat and his hands would tremble when he talked about it. Wave after wave went in, he said, and thousands were mown down."

"Blame the bastards who ordered it," said Davy (Spider) Webb. "What was it that German general said? 'The British troops were lions, but they were led by donkeys'!"

"What you just said, Davy, reminds me of something I read in one of my books about the First World War. It was an extract from a letter written home by a young officer. It said, 'We lost 20,000 men before breakfast this morning, and, by God, with a bit of luck, we'll do the same again tomorrow.'"

"Just bloody cannon fodder!" muttered Davy. "There are ten names on the war memorial at home, and it's only a tiny village where I live. I wonder how many poor devils were killed altogether."

"According to my war books," I said, "we had over 3 million killed and wounded. We also lost about 345,000 horses," I added.

"Poor bloody things!" said Davy. "Why drag them into it? If humans are stupid enough to want to kill each other, all well and good – leave the dumb animals out of it, I say."

"They were the main means of transport," said Allan, "hauling guns and suchlike about."

"Politicians, big-businessmen and arms manufacturers are the people that cause wars," said Davy. "Let them bastards do the fighting, and leave the rest of us out of it!"

"I suppose we in the navy are the best off really," said another member of our little group.

"What do you mean, Taff? We wouldn't be very well off if

we got 'tin-fished' out in the middle of the ocean, would we?"

"No," replied Taff, "but, apart from that or getting hit by a bloody great bomb, we don't need to worry too much, do we? Hand-to-hand fighting with bayonets and hand grenades must be bloody awful. I don't reckon I could do that."

"None of us could until we are directed and ordered to," said Allan. "I reckon Taff has got a point, though: probably most of us will go through the war and never even see one of the enemy."

"Probably most of us hope you are right," said Davy.

Our little party were having a discussion up by the midships pom-poms, looking up towards the barracks.

"According to all we hear and read," said Davy, "the war in Europe won't last much longer. I must be mad to say it, but I think I would rather be on this ship and going out East than be up there [pointing to the barracks]. Do you reckon them poor sods are still pushing brooms around? And do you remember the Gestapo? Put your hat on straight! Turn your collar down! Get your bleeding haircut! Double up, that man! First Lieutenant's report – let's have your station card! What a dump! It wasn't safe to loaf anywhere for more then a couple of minutes. If you did, they were after you."

Two other lads had joined our little gathering. One of them now spoke for the first time. "I got talking to a bloke on my last ship," he said. "He reckoned he never got lumbered for even one job all the time he was in the barracks here."

We all looked at the speaker in disbelief.

"You're pulling our legs," said Davy, "ain't you?"

"No," came the reply. "The way he told it, it was too ridiculous not to be true."

"What did he do," asked Allan, "go to ground? You're not going to ask us to believe he hid up all day and every day!"

"No, sod that for a tale," said Davy. "As we were just saying, the Gestapo were everywhere; there wasn't anywhere to hide."

"He didn't try to hide," said the storyteller. "He did the exact opposite to that."

"You're talking in riddles," I said. "What did he do, then?"

"He walked," was the reply.

"Walked? What do you mean walked? Walked where?"

"Around the barracks all day," was the reply. "It's a fact," he continued. "He had a folder under his arm with papers in it and he just walked from one place to another. Nobody ever said a word to him – that's how he told it."

"He really got away with it?"

"Yes," was the reply. "Never did so much walking in his life before, he said. Seems he had got it worked out to a fine art – had his regular round, so to speak: clothing stores, sickbay (you could always lose yourself there fifteen or twenty minutes), back and forth to the dockyard, several visits to the heads [toilets] each day – naturally! He'd go to various other places sometimes, to throw the Gestapo off the scent if they were watching. You know what the Gestapo are like, he said. You can't trust them bastards! Sometimes he would call down at the main gate, and check the noticeboards; the same down in the drill shed; ship's office; K basement; occasionally the dental surgery. A bit dodgy, that one, he said. Wouldn't do to doze off there or you might suddenly find half your bloody teeth missing!"

"Well, well!" said Davy. "Talk about cheek of the devil – I reckon I have heard everything now."

"I will always remember the first time I fell in for the muster, when men under punishment were piped," remarked Allan. "I thought they must have piped 'clear lower deck' – there were hundreds of blokes there."

"What were you in the rattle for, Allan?" asked Taff.

"Improperly dressed" was the reply. "I should have been wearing my oilskin and wasn't. They made three charges out of that," he added: "improperly dressed, failing to read the noticeboard and failing to comply with the same!"

"I got picked up in the sickbay a couple of times," said one of the newcomers, "and once in the barrack block – when the Gestapo raided it. My oppo [mate] and me sneaked back there a couple of times after the early muster, got out of sight behind the hammock nettings, and crashed our heads down. We thought we were on to a good thing, but it turned out to be 'third time unlucky' – perhaps we had got too greedy! Anyway, the Gestapo decided to make one of their snap raids on the block that particular morning. You blokes will know what they used to do," the speaker continued: "two of the bastards would stand by the door, one at each end, so nobody hiding inside could make a flying escape, and the third one would walk through the block."

"What did you do?" asked Taff.

"Couldn't do anything – caught like rats in a bloody trap, weren't we? 'Well, well,' he says, when he sees us, 'what have we here, then? Shouldn't you two jolly Jack tars be outside on some interesting job or other? Perhaps you have lost track of the time – or never heard the pipe. Maybe you have lost a gold watch or something, or perhaps you're looking for the ship's cat, but I wouldn't believe any of that crap, would I!' You should've seen the smirk on his face, when he says, 'First Lieutenant's report – let's have your cards!'"

"I spent two days here," I said, "when my last ship paid off – before going back to Scotland. You wouldn't believe it, but I was in the rattle before I knew I had done anything wrong."

"What had you done, Matt?" asked Allan.

"I'll tell you," I said. "Several things according to them. I travelled down from South Shields with one of my mates, and they put us in the same mess when we got here. Next morning, the leading hand told us we were cooks for the day. Clean the mess up, fetch the grub from the galley, dish it out, wash up after, etc. – well, you all know how it used to be. There might be a different number of blokes in your mess each time you came to it – they were coming and going all the time, weren't they? Anyway, we were cleaning the table after dinner, getting ready to wash up. There was still some food in the dishes – nobody seemed to want it, and there didn't seem to be anybody else to come, so into the gash bucket it went! Next second, the pair of us nearly jumped out of our skins. 'You two are in the rattle,' a voice roared out behind us. 'Give me your cards.' We wondered what had hit us. There stood the duty petty officer, the OOD and a messenger bloke – all looking at us as though we were bloody criminals!"

"What was it all about, Matt?" asked Davy.

"Wasting food," I replied, "according to them. We mustered with all the other defaulters, and the charges were read out: 'On the umpteenth day of so and so did waste food; did fail to return surplus food to the galley; did fail to carry out duties properly as laid down in Barrack Rules and Regulations; did fail to read barrack notices; did fail to comply with the same. What have you to say in answer to the said charges?'"

"Bloody hell, Matt!" said Allan. "I should think you were speechless."

"What did you think, Matt?" asked Davy. "The firing squad? What did you say?"

"We told them what was, in fact, the truth, Davy: we hadn't been there five minutes, had no time to read the noticeboards, and, as far as we knew, at sea on the small ships no order about returning food ever existed."

"What did they say to that, Matt?"

"They did some muttering among themselves; then the First Lieutenant said, 'Case dismissed.'

"'Case dismissed,' repeated the crusher! 'Watch it, you two! On caps. About turn. Quick march!'"

"You never knew where you were," said Taff. "You daren't relax for a second – all the time looking over your shoulder."

"I hated those tunnels," said Allan. "Remember how it used to be? Lugging your hammock in there every night, and hoping you'd be able to find a place to sling it!"

"I think it was even worse in the mornings, Allan. Scrapping to get your hammock lashed up, with dozens of blokes pushing past you, cursing at one another – all in a mad scramble to get to the wash places and then to the mess for breakfast before it was all gone."

The tunnels at Chatham Barracks were like a rabbit warren – I never knew the full extent of them. They were very well constructed in the hillside at the rear of the four massive barrack blocks. They were well ventilated. I will always remember the draft of cool fresh air and the smell of disinfectant. Arranged along one side of each tunnel were wooden-slatted bunks, and on these early arrivals of men would spread their hammocks. Sleeping like this may not be quite as comfortable as sleeping in a slung hammock, but at least you wouldn't get bumped into all the time as hundreds of later arrivals trooped in, looking for a place to sling. Naturally, the later you arrived, the further in you had to go to find a billet, and you'd be cursed at all the way, as you bumped into people who had already slung their hammocks from the bars in the roof and turned in.

"Watch where you are going, you clumsy bastard!" someone would exclaim, to which the reply would usually be "Get stuffed!" or "Up yours too!"

Many hundreds of men slept in those tunnels every night – indeed, it was a barrack order that everyone had to.

They were also, of course, the barrack air-raid shelters. The loudspeakers would be blaring out one of the hit songs of the day – 'We Three' perhaps, or 'Sierra Sue', or 'There'll Be Bluebirds over the White Cliffs of Dover', and suddenly Vera Lynn would be cut off in the middle of a note. Then we'd hear the urgent order "Air-raid warning RED – take cover!" and there would be an immediate mad scramble for the tunnel entrances. We might be there for just a few minutes, or for half an hour or more. The Tannoy would crackle into life again as the all-clear was sounded. Then maybe it would be 'A Nightingale Sang in Berkeley Square' we were listening to.

The day came when it was time to sail. Numbers had been checked off and heads counted. Mooring wires were cast off and reeled up, fenders were stowed and we were on our way.

The Commander and ship's chaplain paid us a visit a few days later when we were at sea.

"Are you lads happy, being stuck down here?" they asked.

What could we say? There was no point in telling them we hated it. They wouldn't have said, "All right, lads – we will have it dismantled and moved," would they?

"We will manage," we said.

We learned the ship had been out of action for some considerable time earlier in the war. Apparently she had been bombed and set on fire while in dry dock, and the dock had to be flooded, to put the fire out.

On VE day we had just arrived at Malta. There was great excitement among the ruins of Valletta, with everyone flag-waving and celebrating, but we were heading in the wrong direction!

The town itself was no more than a gigantic heap of rubble. It was almost impossible to pick out where a street had been. Malta had suffered innumerable heavy air raids, and the harbour was littered with the wrecks of partly sunken ships. This was the place we ran those supply ships to, from Alexandria, all those years before – the place that had cost the lives of a lot of good men and ships. Maybe some of those wrecks in the harbour were ships we had brought there. We were pleased, naturally, that the war in Europe was over, and especially for the people of Malta. They had had more than their share of it.

As I mentioned earlier, you were likely to meet up with all sorts of characters in wartime service – people with vastly different occupations and backgrounds. On this ship, I knew about two professional musicians, a 'timber feller' from Sevenoaks, a master from one of the 'top' schools, a Birmingham refuse collector, an amateur heavyweight boxing champion, a chap who had been, among other things, a receptionist at the Savoy Hotel, and another who had been 'something in the city'.

There is one character in particular I remember when I think of Malta. He was a Welshman, big and tough, and his battered features told what his occupation had been. He had been sparring partner to Tommy Farr, the pre-war British heavyweight boxing champion. He had also spent a number of years in fairground boxing booths, we learned.

I asked him one day if those fairground fights were genuine, to which he replied, "Some of them were."

I used to go and watch boxing bouts at the Cambridge midsummer fair sometimes. They always drew a good crowd. The showman would stand there delivering his patter – his four or five 'boys' in their dressing gowns ranged alongside him. They always looked pretty bored with the whole thing, I thought. After a while, a suitable challenger would emerge from the crowd and call out, "I'll take one of them on!"

One of the boys of about the same size and weight would be selected, and the showman, who was also the referee, would make the announcement: "If he stops my boy, or lasts for the full three rounds, I will pay him £5. If he gets knocked out himself, or fails to last the three rounds – for any reason whatsoever – then I will pay him nothing. Not one penny piece – not one copper coin!"

The crowd loved it, and they would surge forward to gain admission.

Once the large tent was full to capacity, both men would get gloved up, the challenger having first stripped down to his vest. Round one would be pretty tame – they would be sizing each other up – but perhaps there would be a little flurry of punches at the end of it. Round two would be a bit of a ding-dong, but neither man appeared to get really hurt. The bell would go for round three, but the challenger would be unfit to continue – maybe he had hurt his shoulder.

"But I still think I can beat him!" he would exclaim, and they would be rematched the following night perhaps.

Big Taff got fighting drunk ashore in Malta one night. He wiped the floor with one patrol, and it took a second one to subdue him and bring him back to the ship!

"It doesn't seem natural," said Phil, "lolling around like we are – not a care in the world, so to speak."

"You're dead right, Phil. When I think back to those days – it's all like a dream now."

"A bloody bad dream too," remarked Allan. "I was never so scared in my life before – or since."

"That goes for me too," said Phil, "and, I should imagine, for everybody else who served on Malta convoys. Anyone who says he was not scared is either a liar or a lunatic," he added.

We were midway between Malta and Port Said, and our little group were lying around in the sun chatting. All three of us had been in the Eastern Mediterranean Fleet in the latter half of '41 and early '42. Allan and Phil were in destroyers – not the same ship – and I was with 15th Cruiser Squadron, based at Alexandria.

"Which do you reckon was the worst, Matt: having an action station down below, or on the upper?"

"I don't know, Phil," I replied. "When you are down in a magazine, you wonder all the time what's going on up top; and, of course, if the ship was hit badly and started to sink you might not be able to get out."

"It must have been murder stuck down there," Allan remarked, "but at least you were safe from splinters. When you heard them whining through the air and clattering against the upper works it made you think!"

"I know what you mean, Allan. My action station during one spell was up on the pom-pom deck. Our small party kept the pom-poms supplied, and reloaded the magazines for the Oerlikons. During one action, a lump of steel narrowly missed a couple of us and came to rest against the side of the locker close by. One of the lads examined it when the action was over, and said he thought it was probably part of the base of an AA shell." I looked at Allan and said jokingly, "You were in a 4.5 crew, weren't you? It might have been one of yours – do you realise, you bloody near killed me!"

"I didn't mind the high-level bombers too much," said Phil, "but those bloody Stukas – my guts used to turn to water when they came screaming down. It's a wonder any of us survived," he added; "a lot of poor devils didn't. It was somewhere about here my fair ship was sunk – we could have passed over the exact spot. I wonder how many of the lads are down there with her?"

"You have to forget all that, Matt," said Allan. "It is in the past – put it out of your mind, and just be thankful you were not one of them."

"Yes, I expect you are right," I replied.

"Have either of you two been scared before?" asked Phil. "I mean *really* scared?"

"I was once on Lime Street Station, Liverpool," said Allan, "running the gauntlet of the whores!"

"I know what you mean Allan," I remarked. "I came through there when I came back from the Med. There was a whole swarm of them, grabbing hold of blokes' arms, and trying to lug them off bodily – and the language they came out with when you told them to get lost was nobody's business."

"They were some hard cases all right, Matt. I suppose we all had our scary moments as kids," said Phil. "That's all we were before we joined up, wasn't it? I remember one thing in particular – it's laughable now – just a case of two boys being scared of the dark. I suppose we were about ten or twelve years old, my young pal and me, when we started staying out a bit late in the evenings. Anyway, we lived about half a mile from each other, and the road between our two houses passed by a large wood. It was our playground at weekends, and we spent countless hours there, climbing the trees and making dens and campfires. One day we got a long piece of rope from one of our parents' tool sheds and had a go at being Tarzans! It was a wonder we didn't kill ourselves. In one corner of the wood, close to the road, was a dense mass of privet bushes. At night it appeared as a solid black mass – you could imagine all sorts of things as you walked past it in the dark. Well, one evening, when we were playing in my garden, darkness fell quite suddenly. It sort of caught us unaware.

"'I'm going in now,' I said to my pal. 'See you tomorrow!'

"'I'm scared,' he said, and just stood there.

"'You'll be all right,' I told him. 'There's nothing to be scared about.'

"Well, he started blubbering, and begged me to go part of the way back to his house with him. I didn't particularly want to do that – I reckon we were both thinking about that black patch! However, he persuaded me, and off we went.

"'I'm not scared,' I said.

"I was scared – bloody scared – but I wasn't going to let him know it. When we got opposite the black patch, I started to swank and went quite close to it.

"'Nothing to be scared of here,' I said. 'It doesn't bother me.'

"But I wasn't so bloody brave when I came back alone. My

heart started to bump, and I ran like a hare past that black patch, on the far side of the road and looking straight ahead!"

"I was almost frightened to death once by a bloody great dog," said Allan. "It was a Rhodesian ridgeback – big, nasty bastard. I was an errand boy at a shop for little while when I left school, and I got scared by one or two dogs at different places I went to, but this particular one was a real swine. I came to dread going there. There was a long drive up to this house, and the brute was generally roaming loose in the grounds. Usually it wouldn't take any notice of me going up there; but when I tried to leave, it would come slinking round and stand there in front of my bike, snarling and growling. The old boy would come out and shout and swear at it, and drive it off with a whip, and I would make my escape, so to speak. Well, one day there was no sign of it. I remember thinking, 'I hope the bastard has died!' I dumped the stuff by the back door, got back on the bike and started back. Then I heard it come crashing through the shrubbery. It started barking when it saw me, and my blood ran cold. I glanced over my shoulder and saw it come racing round the corner in great leaps and bounds. I broke out in a cold sweat, put my head down, and pedalled like hell down the drive. I think I prayed to God to let me get to the gates before the brute got to me. Well, I made it by the skin of my teeth. I had left the gate open about three feet – I always did, just in case – and I shot through the gap, half fell off the bike and slammed the gate shut. God, I felt bad! What that brute would have done if it had caught me doesn't bear thinking about. I refused to go there any more."

"How about you, Matt?" asked Phil.

"I remember one incident on the farm that scared me stiff," I replied. "I was only fourteen at the time. The foreman sent me round to the piggeries one morning to 'lend a hand', he said.

"'Perhaps I've got to mix some swill up, or muck some of the sties out,' I thought.

"Many pigs were raised on the farm – there were dozens of them in the yards, and the paddock adjoining, and a man was employed full-time looking after them. This man also looked after and milked the half-dozen or so house cows. Anyway, off I went to the piggeries – unsuspecting.

"'Morning, boy," said old Will – 'Wiggy', we boys called him. He was cross-eyed, so one eye was looking straight into mine, and the other was gazing over my shoulder!

"'You have come to help me, then. I've got the old fella in the sty.'

"'What?' I said.

"'Why – the old boar, boy. Didn't the foreman tell you? You and me are going to trim his old tusks a bit!'

"I didn't want anything to do with boars. I remembered a conversation I had had sometime earlier with old Will, when we boys had been wary of taking our horses through a yard where one of his bulls was.

"'You don't need to worry about an old bull, boy,' he had said. 'When they charge they always shut their eyes just before they get to you – you can always nip to one side out of the way. It's them old boars you want to watch out for. They come at you sideways like a streak of lightning! Nasty sly old devils!'

"I reckon I was looking a bit green about the gills, Phil," I said, "because the old boy put his hand on my shoulder, and said, 'Nothing to be scared about, boy. Come on – let's get on with it.'

"I followed him down the long passageway, a hacksaw and rasp in one hand and a piece of rope in the other. The boar started grunting when he heard our footsteps – or maybe he heard my heart thumping first! He was a big brute, and I didn't like the look in his mean little eyes. I didn't want to go in that sty with him."

"I reckon I would have scarpered there and then," Allan broke in.

"Yeah – me too," echoed Phil. "What happened then, Matt?"

"Well," I said, "the old boy asked me to hold the tools while he opened the sty door, and I thought I had been reprieved when he said, 'You don't need to come in, boy.' Then, when he turned to shut it, he gave a little grin and said, 'Not yet!'"

"The old sod!" said Phil. "He was winding you up, Matt. What happened then?"

"He made a loop in the rope," I replied, "a sort of a running noose – maybe it was a bowline on the bight."

"Never mind what kind of knot it was," said Phil; "get on with the story!"

"All right, Phil," I said. "This is what the old boy said to me: 'I'm going to slip this loop over the old chap's top jaw; then we'll pull his head up to the side of the fence and tie it there. You go round into the next sty, boy, and I'll pass the end over to you.'

"I did as he directed – took the rope over the top rail, and passed the end back to him. We hauled away, and up came the boar's head – half a foot or so.

"'That should do,' said old Will, and made the rope fast round the top rail." I looked at Phil, and said, "I'm not sure whether it was a clove hitch, rolling hitch or fisherman's bend!"

"Maybe it was a round turn and two half-hitches, Matt," said Allan with a glance at Phil.

Phil didn't say anything – just stood there grinning.

"'Right, boy – in here now. Get hold of that top rail over his back, push your knees hard into his old gut, and hold him there!'

"I did that, trembling like a leaf, and old Will got down on his hands and knees and began sawing and rasping away. His head was quite close to the boar's, and I couldn't help wondering what would happen if that bit of rope were to break. It didn't look very strong, and the boar kept jerking his head.

"However, it didn't break, and after a while – it seemed hours to me, but was probably just a few minutes – old Will said, 'I think that will do for now. Right, boy – out you get.'"

"I bet you were pleased to hear that, Matt!"

"You can say that again, Allan," I replied.

"'Leave the sty door open wide, boy, and open the door into the yard – he can go straight outside then.'

"I did that and went into the safety of the next sty – I wasn't sure what the boar would do when he was released. The old boy took a knife from his pocket, opened it up, and pushed the blade under the rope on top of the boar's snout. A quick jerk, back and up, and the boar was free – he went out like a shot out of a gun hollering and shaking his head from side to side.

"Old Will looked at me, gave a sly little grin, and said, 'I bet he were more scared than you were, boy.'

"'I wouldn't bet on it,' I thought."

"I bet you were pleased when it was over," said Allan.

"You can say that again," I replied. "Old Will died a month or two later, and his son Harry took over the job. Queer bloke he was – very moody. He didn't want to speak to anybody at times, and often when he did he would snap your head off. He used to curse the cows something terrible when they wouldn't do what he wanted. If they didn't come when he called them, we could hear him plainly from our garden – a quarter of a mile away.

"'Shut up, you leary bugger!" my father would shout.

"'I expect it's the malaria,' my mother used to say.

"Harry had spent several years in the army in India."

"Do you reckon you will go back on the farm, Matt, when this lot is over?"

"I don't know," I replied. "Haven't really thought about it. There's not a lot of choice where I come from. Apart from farming, there is the railway and the local council, or maybe I could get a job in a shop in town. That about sums it up, I think. There is nothing in the way of industry. I don't have any trade or qualifications."

"How about going into the racing stables?" suggested Phil. "Do you fancy that?"

"No," I said. "I liked the working horses on the farm, but I'm not in the least interested in racing, or any other kind of horsey event."

"Can't see myself going back to my old job," remarked Allan. "It was in a cycle repair shop – imagine standing there all day and every day, putting spokes back in wheels what some stupid kid has knocked out, mending punctures, straightening bent mudguards . . . It would drive me up the wall now."

"I don't fancy my old job either," said Phil: "coal merchant's yard, weighing the stuff and helping to load it on the lorries. Dirty bloody job too! But I'll have plenty of time to think about it – the war ain't over yet!"

"I wish those bastard Japs had packed it in when the Jerries did – we wouldn't have to be going out there, then."

"I thought for a minute in the drafting office at *Osprey,* Phil, I was going to get out of it. When the sub lieutenant there asked me if I had done any previous foreign service, I said yes almost before he had finished asking the question. I thought I was going to get out of the draft, but I soon came down to earth again when he asked how long I had been back in the UK. I was tempted to say, 'About six months,' but knew I would never get away with it. 'Two and a half years,' I said.

"Well, he gave a little lopsided grin and replied, 'Oh, I think you won't mind going again.'

"'Thank you very much!' I thought. 'I wonder how long you have been sat here on your arse. I wonder if you have done any foreign service!'"

"Can't win them all," said Allan.

We had passed through the canal and were on our way down the Red Sea. There was still much speculation as to where we were headed for. One buzz said somewhere in South East Asia Command, and another said to the Pacific theatre – to help the Yanks out.

Up till now, I personally had had only two close encounters with our American allies. The first of these had been in Durban, when I was on my way back to the UK from the Malta convoys. An American ship had called in at the port – probably her first trip across, as they had been in the war only a few weeks. Anyway, several of us were sitting in a bar, having a quiet drink and chatting together, when two Yankee sailors appeared in the doorway.

They stood there gazing around at us, then one of them drawled, "We've had thirty-two days at sea, and we come here and find the British Navy loafing around boozing!"

A frozen silence greeted the unfortunate remark. One of our lads – wearing an AA gunner's badge on his sleeve – got slowly to his feet from a nearby table. He took a few steps and his fist crashed into the American's jaw – and he went head over heels backwards out of the door! The other American stood as if rooted to the spot with his mouth hanging half open. When he was asked if he had any comment to make about the Royal Navy, he quickly turned and left.

The other encounter was in a small French fishing port. It was a few days after leaving Devonport Dockyard, after the repairs to our damaged side. A Yankee cutter came and tied up alongside us, and a small party of our lads were chatting to one of the crew.

"I'm a radar man," he informed us.

Apparently they had been patrolling around the Channel Islands area, and had a skirmish with E-boats.

"We had one hell of a bad time!"

"Can't see any damage," we said. "How many times were you hit?"

"Oh, we didn't actually get hit," he replied.

"Many casualties?" we asked.

"No – none of the guys were hurt, but we had a hell of a bad time!"

He was joined by one of his shipmates, whom he greeted with "Howdy, Al – what gives?"

We chatted together for a bit, and then the newcomer moved off.

"Is he a radar man too?" we asked.

"Heck, no!" was the reply. "Al is our commander!"

We couldn't visualise British sailors being on even conversational terms with their commander, let alone calling him by his first name. The divide was too great.

The Southeast Asia Command buzz proved to be the correct one. Colombo, the capital of what was then called Ceylon, was to be our base.

We went out on patrol almost immediately – without incident – and then called in at Trincomalee, on the other side of the island. It was while we were there that the class thing reared its ugly head again, in the form of a notice that appeared on the boards one morning. It was headed, 'RE BATHING OVER THE SIDE'. I should have mentioned that when in sheltered waters, and when the situation permitted, the crew were allowed to bathe over the ship's side. Swimming was very popular with many of the lads – the duty boat being in attendance in case anyone got into difficulties. The notice went on to say, 'The ship's company is hereby informed that the water abaft the whaler's davits [roughly one-third of the ship's length] shall be reserved for officers only.' There was nearly a riot when we read it.

"Those - - - - pigs!" was the general comment. "They're trying to segregate the bloody ocean now!"

One lad ripped the notice down, screwed it up, threw it down on the deck and trampled on it.

"I like to swim right round the ship," he said, "and those bastards ain't going to stop me."

"They can tell me what to do on the ship," said another. "I accept that – but when I'm off it, and swimming in the ocean, those bloody pigs tell me nothing!"

"If we get 'tin-fished' and have to swim for it, do you reckon that order will still apply?" remarked another lad. "If that ever does happen," he added, "and I find any pigs swimming round our end, I'll drown the bastards!"

The order was ignored, and no more was heard about it.

The mail from home caught up with us when we returned to Colombo a few days later, and I was very pleased to find two letters from Jeannie for me. Apparently she had been drafted herself soon after I had left, and her second letter bore an address down on the English Channel coast.

She wrote, 'I am not very happy about it, but I must not complain as I had a good long spell at the old place.' She went on to say, 'I am so lucky really – Meg has come with me. Wonders never cease!'

We did another patrol – quite uneventful and boring. Everyone was heartily sick of the war by now, and we all hoped it would end quickly.

We compared notes on our lives before the war, and came to the conclusion that none of us had been anywhere or experienced anything of note.

I thought back to my childhood years, when we sometimes went on summer holidays to my aunt's, in a small village near Martlesham Aerodrome. It was the main experimental base for the RAF, and my uncle was employed there. He would tell me sometimes when a brand-new aircraft would be arriving to be put through its paces by one of the test pilots. I recall when a huge monoplane arrived at the base – it must have been about 1930, I should think. Its landing wheels were a staggering seven feet in diameter, and I believe I am correct in saying that it was the largest single-wing aircraft in the world at that time.

I had a special thrill at my aunt's house one holiday. I was sitting in the house reading a book when I heard my aunt calling me from the garden. She sounded very excited, and when I dashed outside she pointed to a huge airship which was travelling very slowly over the airfield. Even as we watched, it altered course towards us and passed almost directly overhead. It was quite low, and we could plainly see figures in the gondola. On the side, in huge letters, was the name *Graf Zeppelin*. It circled the base twice then flew off. Years later, when the war came, we wondered if it had been taking photographs.

I was to see another airship a few years later. We were in the old farm cottage one evening when we heard the sound of engines. That was an event in itself, as we seldom, if ever, heard a vehicle of any kind on the farm road at night. The sound swelled into a roar, and we dashed outside just in time to see a huge airship passing overhead. We heard on the radio, the next morning, the sad news that the R101 had crashed in France.

It was at my aunt's that I had my first cigarette. I had been pestering my uncle to let me try one, and I expect he got so fed up that he finally relented.

"All right," he said, "in the old privy, out of sight. Don't let your aunt know or she will bloody kill me!"

It was an event when Aunt Charlotte came to tea. Everyone called her that. I think she was my aunt's aunt really, but I don't know for sure. She was a very prim and fussy little lady, and I had to be on my very best behaviour when she was there. She came once a month, arriving punctually at four o'clock on her tricycle. There was a very steep hill running past my aunt's house, and once or twice we thought she would go sailing straight past when she came down it!

At this period, my eldest sister used to come on holiday with me, and it would be our duty to push Aunt Charlotte back up the hill when she left punctually at six thirty. She would thank us profusely and give us a silver sixpence between us!

It was an event also when my aunt took us to Ipswich on the bus, and to Felixstowe on the Bluebird charabanc. All that was many years ago, but I remember it clearly.

I also remember race weeks at Newmarket, and watching the great steam engines that brought the special trains down from London – twelve or fourteen carriages on some of them. We saw the *Flying Scotsman*, *Royal Scot*, and *Duchess of Sutherland*, among others, several times. As a matter of interest, Newmarket Station had some of the longest platforms in the country at that time to accommodate the race trains.

Some of my mates in the navy thought it quite odd that I hadn't been employed in the racing stables – coming from Newmarket, as I did. However, I have never had much interest in horse events of any kind, and have only been on Newmarket Racecourse a couple of times in my whole life. I certainly never got involved in betting on horses. That truly is a mug's game. Too many people in Newmarket knew of a good thing – a red-hot tip to pass on. Those that really knew, I think, kept it to themselves. Betting on horses can get to be an expensive habit; it is almost a disease with some people.

This reminds me of a little story about a former stable lad I got to know. A few years after the war, I was scratching a living from a little plant nursery I had built up – supplying one of the hotels in town with salad stuff in the season, and a shop with cut flowers and pot plants. Adjoining my bit of ground, which I rented, was a small pig-and-poultry concern belonging to a retired trainer. His house was nearby, and he employed one of his former stablemen to run it. Many a time little Fred came round to my greenhouse on a Monday morning to scrounge a cigarette.

"Didn't you get paid last week?" I would ask.

"Yes," he would reply, "but I spent Saturday afternoon in the bookmakers, didn't I?"

"Why don't you pack it in, Fred?" I said to him once. "You know it's a mug's game."

"I can't," he replied. "I've got to have my bet."

I had quite an amusing conversation with little Fred one day – some time later. It was the occasion of his boss's daughter's wedding day. A small paddock to the rear, next to Fred's department, was the car park for the guests.

About the middle of the afternoon, Fred gave me a shout: "Come here a minute – I want to show you something." I strolled round and joined him, and he said, "You see that smashing Jaguar – well, I'm a part-owner."

"What do you mean, Fred?" I asked.

"It's my bookmaker's," he said. "I helped buy it!"

One wise character I knew summed it all up like this: if you can say to yourself at the end of the season, "I haven't lost anything," you can say you have had a good season.

My father was very good with horses. One of his jobs was groom to the boss's old hunter. He had been with a cavalry regiment in the early part of the First World War, and I recall him telling us as children how in 1916 he had become a rough-rider. They broke wild horses and mules in and taught men to ride; they also broke them to harness, for gun-carriage and limber teams.

My mother had a card at home – one of those novelty Christmas cards Father had sent from France. It depicted in a number of pen-and-ink sketches aspects of a rough-rider's job, and the progress being made: wild horses being rounded up in the Argentine, driven on to ships, and unloaded in France, and various stages of the breaking-in process. There were sketches of men being bitten, kicked from various angles, pulled over and trampled on, etc. Other sketches showed men learning to ride: getting thrown off, climbing back on, clutching two handfuls of mane, hanging on for dear life, and hanging upside down beneath the horse's neck! The final sketch was of a team of six, in three pairs, hauling a heavy gun through the mud with a mounted rough-rider on the near side of each pair, urging them on.

Father was not particularly big, but he was a tough old boy. I don't ever recall him showing any emotion about anything. Having said that, however, maybe there was just one occasion – but even then I'm not really sure. It was when I arrived home unexpectedly from the Malta convoys in early May 1942. I thought there were tears in his eyes as we talked, but I'm not sure.

Father's forebears were gamekeepers and warreners; my mother's were shepherds. She was a soft and gentle person. Her parents originated from Long Melford in Suffolk, and thereby hangs a little story – two, in fact. Mother's maiden name was Ramsey, and, from odd pieces of information that came to light, she became convinced that our family was related to that of Alf Ramsey, the manager of Ipswich Town Football Club at that time – later he became Sir Alf Ramsey, the England manager. I think she may well have been right.

Mother often spoke about an uncle of hers who had a wagon-building business at Long Melford. His name was Alfred Ward. A few years ago – about 1984, I suppose it would be – I was clearing up a rough corner in what had been a farmyard, close to our home at Thurlow, near Haverhill, when I came upon some rusty and partly decayed ironwork. I immediately recognised it as part of a farm wagon or cart, and presently I unearthed a flat rectangular piece, about six inches by twelve inches. After scrubbing and chipping the rust and clay away, I saw that it was a maker's nameplate. It bore the name and inscription:

Alfred Ward, Wagon builder
Long Melford, Suffolk.

In early August the buzz said we would be going on the offensive.

The following afternoon we fired what must have been some of the last naval shells to be fired in anger in the Second World War. Japanese military installations on the west coast of Malaya were the target. We lobbed about sixty eight-inch shells at them, without reply; then there was an AA alarm. Two Japanese planes had been sighted – the first of which was shot down almost immediately by a direct hit from the four-inch gun, it was thought. The plane was seen to disintegrate completely. The ship had a very heavy AA armament, and the barrage put up was quite spectacular. The second plane made a wide circle right round us, then suddenly turned directly towards the ship, quite low down.

Probably everyone thought the same as I did: 'It's one of those kamikazes and it's going to crash on to the ship!'

As I was in the anti-submarine branch, I did not have an AA action station, so thought I would stay up top and watch the action. Stupid perhaps, with bullets and cannon shells flying about from our escorting destroyers – but I had some protection overhead, where I was standing! I was on the torpedo-tube deck midships, on the upper deck. The deck here was open on each side for the tubes to be trained round, but covered overhead. Immediately above me was one of the eight eight-barrel pom-poms.

I lay flat on the deck as the plane still came on. There was an absolute torrent of fire going out at it. The noise was deafening, and the sea all around and below the plane was a forest of splashes, from shells and shell fragments. Still it came on, about fifty feet above the water. Then the pom-poms began hitting. Pieces flew off the wings; then, a few seconds later, a stream of flame came from the fuselage. Still it came on, lower now – just the wing stubs and fuselage. All the firing stopped when it was about fifty yards away – the guns were on maximum depression.

Every man was holding his breath, I imagined. Would it hit us?

It hit the water, bounced a couple of times (which reduced its speed considerably), bumped almost gently into our side – and sank. There was no explosion, thankfully, and only minor damage was done to the ship's side.

I was talking to some of the pom-pom crew afterwards, and

one of them told me they had seen the pilot crouched in his cockpit, his arms folded before his face.

A day or two later, we heard news that stunned us: the atom bombs had been dropped on Japan.

The war was over – almost.

When the Japanese made their lightning conquest of Singapore, a member of our small village community was on the last ship to get away. I was to be on the first ship to return, and the Japanese surrender of the area was signed on board my ship. I can see those high-ranking Japanese officers now, strutting about on board in their immaculate uniforms, faces inscrutable, ceremonial swords at their sides.

Ashore I saw what they had been responsible for when we opened up Changi gaol and other internment camps. They were inhuman, and we let them off too lightly, I think.

Singapore was a fascinating place, we thought. It had all the mysteries of the East to us younger lads.

One of my memories – quite a ridiculous one really – is of loads of brand-new banknotes blowing around in the street. Young lads were pushing whole bundles of Japanese-issued notes into our hands for a few cigarettes. The moment the Japanese surrendered, their money became worthless, of course.

A strong buzz began the rounds: the commander-in-chief was coming! A guard of honour was paraded on the quay, waiting and waiting and waiting. Two or three chaps collapsed with heat exhaustion, and others, including me, were getting pretty near to it, I think, when he finally arrived. A quick walk along the ranks of men, a glance at one here and there, and he was gone again. Was it all worth it? we wondered. I think he couldn't have cared less about all the pomp and ceremony.

They came on board the next day – the great man and his lady. Several of the lads were lying around in various stages of undress, sunbathing, and they scrambled to their feet when they saw our distinguished visitors.

"No need," he said, smiling. "Relax!"

They stayed on board for some time, chatting to groups of

men. Many of our crew were just sprogs – eighteen- and nineteen-year-olds; I myself had become one of the senior ABs, with five years' service behind me.

Noticing the badges on my arms, he said, "You'll have got some sea time in – where have you been spending it?"

I mentioned Atlantic convoys and, before that, Malta convoys. He became very interested, and asked what ship I had been on. When I replied, "The cruiser flagship," he said, "You will have known the Mad Admiral, then!"

"Yes," I replied; "well, not personally, sir."

Lord Louis had been with the Eastern Mediterranean Fleet at that time as a destroyer captain.

We spent a couple of weeks at Singapore, with plenty of shore leave, but meanwhile trouble was brewing in Java, in the Dutch East Indies. Apparently the Indonesians wanted the Dutch out. We went to the south. We might have to evacuate European women and children, we were informed.

The ship's carpenters and numerous helpers began partitioning off some of the mess decks, and constructing temporary showers and toilets, etc.

We stopped engines on the equator for a couple of hours or so for the 'crossing the line' ceremony. This had been suspended, of course, while the war was on; and although I had previously crossed and recrossed several times this was to be the official initiation. We were duly shaved, etc. and ducked in a portable canvas swimming pool. I have the certificate scroll hanging on my wall still.

It was a rather comic situation ashore in Batavia and Surabaya. The Japanese – our defeated enemy – had been permitted to keep their arms, and were guarding various installations and properties. We had become temporary allies. Every Jap we passed came to attention, then bowed deeply.

I never knew if the planned evacuation of civilians took place, because it was here in Java that my long journey back to Civvy Street began. My age-and-service group number came through one morning, and I was given about an hour and a half to pack my gear and board a destroyer bound for Singapore. Then I had to wait three weeks for transport from Singapore to Ceylon, which turned out to be an aircraft carrier.

We travelled across Ceylon by train from Trincomalee, the naval base, to Colombo. It was a thoroughly enjoyable journey, and we actually saw elephants at work, moving huge tree trunks.

I was to spend another frustrating three weeks in a camp in Colombo before embarking one morning on the cruiser HMS *London* for the last leg of the journey back to Chatham Dockyard.

We spent Christmas day in the Red Sea, of all places. A special Christmas dinner menu was printed and distributed to all ranks. I kept it for a number of years, but it eventually got lost.

It was a cold, wet and miserable morning when we nosed into Chatham Dockyard and berthed alongside. I had been at this exact spot just once before, and on this very same ship. The wheel had turned full circle.

"We are going to miss all this," the chap standing alongside me remarked. "What we have been through these last few years! It is going to seem pretty flat in Civvy Street, I reckon," he added.

"I have been thinking that myself," I said: "all the excitement and adventure, all the good times and the bad, being together, risking our lives together, all depending on one another."

Nothing else in this life can remotely compare with it. All the men and women who served in the services during the war will know exactly what I mean; those who didn't probably can't begin to understand.

When we had completed the demob routine, a large notice stared us in the face on the inside of the last door to Civvy Street. It said, 'It Is Still Not Too Late to Re-enlist'!

"How about you, Jack?" said the petty officer sitting at the desk. "Fancy a few more years?"

"I don't think I will bother," I said. "It wouldn't be the same as before."

CHAPTER 11

BONNIE SCOTLAND (III):
OLD FOOTSTEPS

I never saw Jeannie again. After many, many years, I went on holiday to the place where we met. It looked rather different from what I remembered, but I suppose it would after such a long time. I previously only saw the place in the dark, dull days of winter; and in wartime, of course, everything looked drab and grey.

Walking along the front from the hotel, I tried to remember exactly where my old base stood. The actual buildings were probably pulled down long ago, I supposed, but I was determined to find the site. A little further along, I stopped dead in my tracks. That little wooden landing stage ahead – surely that is where we used to get the ferry. Obviously unused now, it looked very forlorn. It was rotting away, and part of it had in fact collapsed. I stood there for a few minutes, thinking back to those days. This is where I said goodbye to this little town – it had been a very sad parting. I thought of my old friend Allan, one of the best mates I had in the service.

"You will be coming back here, Matt!" he had said.

'You were right, Allan,' I thought, 'but it has taken a long time – and then not in the way you thought.'

Then there was Alf, the Londoner. I wonder if he settled the account outside the *Pembroke* gate? Rough, tough lads, some of those Londoners!

When we came ashore here we turned left and then took one of the side roads, which led straight up to the base – but how far, and which one? I couldn't decide, so selected one at random. After a few minutes' walk I came to a junction – my base had stood on the corner of a junction just like this one, and I was pretty sure this road would lead down to the centre of this little town. There was no landmark I recognised, so I tried another junction then retraced my steps back in the other direction. That was no good, so I decided to ask someone. A quite elderly gentleman was approaching, walking his dog.

'Just the ticket!' I said to myself. 'He looks as though he is a local resident.'

"Pardon me, but I wonder if you could help me."

I explained my quest, and he replied, "I remember it well, laddie, but those old buildings were demolished years ago!"

"I expected they would have been," I said, "but I hoped to find the site."

"You are on the right road," he said, "but it was further down towards the town. Look for the junction with Kings Road – that is where it was. A school building now occupies part of the site," he added.

I thanked him and said, "It's not good to look back, is it?"

"That's what they say, laddie," he replied. "You will find yourself doing it more and more as you get older." He laughed and added, "When you are eighty-two, what is there to look forward to!"

I couldn't think of any reply to that, so thanked him again and went on my way.

No problem now – after 400 yards or so, and three junctions, I was there. I stood at the spot where I judged our entrance gates had stood, and pictured in my mind the old buildings. It had been a cosy, friendly little base – the least pusser of any I stayed at. Parties of us lads spent several hours outside here, I recalled, clearing snow and ice from the road and pavements during that sharp winter of '44/5.

There is not a stick left of it now – there is nothing left of any of my old bases.

HMS *Ganges* was closed down several years ago, and has now become a marina, I believe. HMS *Pembroke*, the naval barracks at Chatham, is no more. Of the three ships I served on, the first lies at the bottom of the Med, and the other two went to the breaker's yard a few years after the war ended – all gone. Nothing is left but memories – some of those are best forgotten, but a few others (very special ones) will always remain.

I had been here on two occasions all those years before – once for a few days only, and the second time for eight or ten weeks or so – half of which I had spent at the Glentoran.

'Shouldn't be too difficult to find that,' I thought, but here again my memory was not quite as good as I thought. It was larger and further out on the edge of town than I remembered it. Standing on high ground, gleaming white in the sunlight, it looked very impressive; but, of course, I had never before seen the place by daylight. It was still quite dark when I came down in the mornings on the school bus, and again when I left in the late afternoon.

'That row of windows just below the red tiled roof – they had been the girls' rooms. Now, which one had been Jeannie's?' The second or third from the left – she had told me, but I couldn't remember which it was.

I pictured the kitchen as I had known it – I don't suppose I would recognise it now.

I wonder where all the girls are today. Perhaps they have had reunions – lots of ex-service people did after the war. I found I could recall all their faces quite clearly – how young we all were then!

I thought of Jessie – Chatterbox. When she explained the potato-peeling machine to me, that first morning, "Don't leave them in too long," she had said, "or they will come out like marbles!" Such a nice girl, Jessie – kind-hearted and understanding. I thought of Meg, Helen and the others, and of course Jeannie – a little bundle of fun. There were often excited voices and laughter when she was around.

The girls all thought Chief was an old dragon, but she wasn't at all really. "I think the world of them," she said to me one day, "but I would never let them know that."

Mam Spam – the catering officer – I wonder what kind of

person she was. I never did meet her.

I enjoyed my stay at the Glentoran. I shall always remember it as a happy place – sitting out the back, listening to the girls' chatter or someone singing as I picked the eyes out of potatoes, opened tins or cleaned fish, etc. 'Let Him Go, Let Him Tarry' seems to have been someone's favourite, I recall. Maybe the kitchen still echoes to the girls' laughter.

An amusing thought came to me: 'Suppose I went in there now, marched up to the reception and said, "Is it all right if I go and have a look at your kitchen?" I wonder what they would say. Probably tell me to get lost, I should think, but of course they would understand, wouldn't they?

There was just one more spot for me to visit now. It was quite close to the Glentoran. I crossed the junction and came to a halt. This was it – this was our meeting place. We used to be so pleased when we met and went for our walks. Even bitterly cold nights – snowing at times – didn't worry us. I suppose we were little more than children then really. From the junction a road leads down to the loch side, where we used to go for our walks.

A few weeks ago, when turning out the drawers of an old sideboard, I came across some picture postcards Jeannie had sent me after the war. They showed places she had visited on holiday outings, etc., and included with them was a view from across the loch where we used to go walking. On the back she had written just three words: 'Remember this place?'

It seems a long time ago – it is all back in the dim and distant past, a lifetime ago.

Sadly, it was also on this spot that we said goodbye. Dear little Jeannie – where are you now? She told me in her letters that she would be visiting friends here after the war – I wonder if she sometimes came back to the spot. I guess that is something I will never know. Maybe Jeannie *still* visits there. Maybe she was there on that day. Maybe we passed on the street and didn't know it. That raises an interesting question: if we were to meet, would we even recognise each other after all these years? I guess I will never know the answer to that either.

Aloud, I said, "It's time to go."

A police car had passed by a few minutes earlier with a very young-looking officer at the wheel. If he had come back and found me still standing there, he might have thought I was behaving suspiciously – loitering with some dubious purpose or other in mind.

The thought amused me – but of course I knew he wouldn't understand how I felt about the place. I suppose to him the war was something that happened way back in history.

As I stood there, thinking my thoughts, the police car reappeared. It stopped about twenty-five yards past where I was standing. The driver got out, and came walking towards me.

'He doesn't look much more than a lad,' I thought – 'a keen lad, curious to know what I'm doing here!'

"Good morning, sir," he said. "Can I be of assistance?"

"No, I don't think so, thank you," I replied.

"You are a stranger here?"

"I suppose you could say that, officer – although I have been here before."

I don't know what he was thinking, but there was a puzzled look on his face.

"I noticed you when I came down, sir – waiting for someone perhaps?"

'The lad is definitely keen,' I thought – 'I will string him along a bit!'

"I had an arrangement to meet a friend here."

We chatted for a few minutes, then he said he had better be getting on his way. "Doesn't look as though your friend is coming, sir – or perhaps you were late arriving," he added with a little smile.

"I think you are right, officer," I replied. "I was late – about forty years late."

A startled expression came to his face when I said that. I couldn't help smiling.

"Don't be alarmed," I said. "There is a simple explanation. I was based here many years ago – during the war – and I'm just reliving old memories, retracing old footsteps."

That seemed to satisfy him – he looked quite relieved. We chatted for another minute or two, then went our separate ways.

I took a last look over my shoulder before I turned the corner, and the Glentoran was gone; but I will always remember it – and this little town and Jeannie.

If ever Jeannie should read my story, perhaps she too will remember.

The happiest part of my wartime service in the Royal Navy was spent at this place, so I think it fitting that my story ends here – just one more coincidence.